SURVEILLANCE AFTER
SNOWDEN

SURVEILLANCE AFTER SNOWDEN

DAVID LYON

POLITY

The right of David Lyon to be identified as Author of this Work
has been asserted in accordance with the UK Copyright, Designs and
Patents Act 1988.

First published in 2015 by Polity Press
Reprinted 2015 (twice)

Polity Press
65 Bridge Street
Cambridge CB2 1UR, UK

Polity Press
350 Main Street
Malden, MA 02148, USA

ISBN-13: 978-0-7456-9084-1
ISBN-13: 978-0-7456-9085-8(pb)

A catalogue record for this book is available from the British Library.

Lyon, David, 1948-
Surveillance after Snowden / David Lyon.
pages cm
Includes bibliographical references and index.
(pbk.) ISBN 978-0-7456-9084-1 (hardback) – ISBN 978-0-7456-9085-8
control.   1. Privacy, Right of.   2. Electronic surveillance.   3. Social
1983-   7.4. Data protection.   5. Civil rights.   6. Snowden, Edward J.,
Official secrets–United States.   8. Government information–
United States.   I. Title.
JC596.L959 2015
323.44′8–dc23

Typeset in 10.75 on 14 pt Adobe Janson
by Toppan Best-set Premedia Limited
Printed and bound in the United States by RR Donnelley

The publisher has used its best endeavours to ensure that the URLs for
external websites referred to in this book are correct and active at the time of
going to press. However, the publisher has no responsibility for the websites
and can make no guarantee that a site will remain live or that the content is or
will remain appropriate.

Every effort has been made to trace all copyright holders, but if any have been
inadvertently overlooked the publisher will be pleased to include any necessary
credits in any subsequent reprint or edition.

For further information on Polity, visit our website: politybooks.com

CONTENTS

PREFACE

This is a book about surveillance, lit up brilliantly by revelations made by Edward Snowden. Since he started to release documents taken from the National Security Agency we know much more about global mass surveillance. It spreads invisibly, capturing gargantuan amounts of personal information from ordinary citizens in its data dragnet. Governments scramble to come to terms with the revelations, sometimes sparking serious policy responses, sometimes diverting attention from the issues or dismissing Snowden as misguided and worse.

Snowden's concern is surveillance, an ancient set of practices but a very prominent means of power today. Governments, corporations, police, indeed organizations of whatever kind, make use of surveillance, intentionally or unintentionally, for good or ill. Surveillance has seeped so far into the very arteries, the capillaries of culture, that it is often seen as an unquestioned requirement of modern life.

The Snowden revelations, although they are clearly about high-level surveillance carried out by security and intelligence agencies, also reflect this resort to surveillance in many contexts. Surveillance occurs in the most high-tech ways and at the pinnacles of power but depends on the humdrum, mundane communications and exchanges that we all make using online media and communication devices such as cellphones. The little messages in tweets and posts are connected with international security in ways that would have been unimaginable to the surveillance novelists and commentators of yesterday.

Some have lauded Snowden as a whistleblower. In the US, former security officers from the NSA, CIA, FBI and the Justice Department recognized his work with the Sam Adams award in October 2013. He also won the 2013 Whistleblower Award in Germany[1] and Sweden's alternative Nobel Prize, the Right Livelihood Honorary Award in 2014.[2] Snowden has quickly become known everywhere as a controversial figure who dared speak out against mass surveillance in a post-9/11 world. A global public now has surveillance on its radar as never before.

However, at a time when terrorist attacks are frequently in the news – one thinks of the Boston Marathon bombing in 2013 or the Paris attacks on the staff of satirical magazine *Charlie Hebdo* in 2015 – government reflexes, amplified by shrill media, call for more surveillance, more security. While urgent action is indeed vital to prevent such appalling bloodshed, this book shows that the kinds of mass surveillance Snowden has revealed at the NSA do not work and also carry major risks for ordinary citizens. This suggests that it is more, not less, important to heed Snowden at a time of intensified attacks.

This book is one kind of response. It aims to place the Snowden revelations in context. It shows how our apparently inconsequential little routines and habits and our very life-chances are affected – especially when the social group to which we belong is a minority or for some reason is already singled out for special treatment. And it highlights how surveillance enables or constrains our ability to live freely in democratic societies. So knowing about it – what it is, who practises it and why, and what difference it makes to our lives – is extremely important. As an academic I believe passionately that the fruit of our work should be open and available to the public and also that it should be clear about where it is coming from and what sorts of values it espouses.

So let me come out with it here. Surveillance raises questions of analysis, yes, but also, unavoidably, of politics and ethics. On the analysis side, the issues are huge because they concern global power alignments that skew surveillance in negative ways. The internet is itself a key arena where this plays out. But the sheer scope of the issues is not an excuse for despair, withdrawal or complacency. Human beings are still active agents who can make a difference, especially when they work in concert. Look no further than Edward Snowden, aged just 29, who rocked the world. There are grounds for hope.

On the politics-and-ethics side – they are the other face of the coin whose analytic face I just sketched – surveillance is a site of struggle, of controversy. Its currency is terms such as privacy, civil liberties, human rights. Each of these is profoundly ethical and thus confronts us with questions that are unavoidably philosophical and even spiritual as well as political. What rights do government bodies, the police, or other organizations have to gain access to our private, personal or intimate lives? What are the limits to using categories of suspicion to name someone who may have committed a crime? Why should anyone care about what is done with personal data?

This book takes us from some world-historic events that continue to make headlines to the trends that underlie them and then to the deeper questions lying below the surface. How do I approach these? I acknowledge and try to be aware of what influences my work. I live in Canada, and of course geography affects one's outlook. I write not only as someone interested in the headlines – a citizen – and in explaining trends – a sociologist – but also as one who identifies as a believer, in my case a Christian. This is not the place to explain more fully how this works out in practice, but I have tried to indicate elsewhere why I do what I do in the way I do and if you are interested, please check it out.[3]

On the trends and sociology side, I have included notes for you to check things for yourself, if you wish, but I have not discussed theory. If that is what you are looking for, the underlying explanations are implied in the text and explored in the works to which the notes refer. I know that for many, the important thing is to get a sense of why there is such a widespread and heated response to the Snowden revelations, what the disclosed documents mean and what can be done about them in an everyday context as well as in law and policy.

My contribution aims to show why Snowden's revelations are so significant, by exposing and exploring the conditions that gave rise to the kinds of surveillance specific to the twenty-first century. What is happening in the world of digital communications that connects our daily doings with worldwide flows of power? What legal limits, policies and practices already exist to help us and what new attitudes and actions are called for?

I deliberately juxtapose the global with the personal, the structural with the active, to show just what the dangers of mass surveillance are and how they can be countered and curbed. It is a call to realism about the risks, which are tremendous, but also to action that might turn the tide. The future is not foreclosed by technology, government or corporate power. However, we can be sure that their negative impacts are enabled by complacency.

Notes

1 The award presented every two years by the Vereinigung Deutscher Wissenschaftler and the German Section of the International Association of Lawyers against Nuclear Arms.
2 See V. Kessler, 'Edward Snowden wins Sweden's "Alternative Nobel Prize"', Reuters, 24 Sept. 2014, at http://in.reuters.com/article/2014/09/24/sweden-snowden-award-nobel-idINKCN0HJ1O920140924/.
3 See, as a starting point, D. Lyon, 'Surveillance and the eye of God', *Studies in Christian Ethics* 27.1 (2014): 1–12.

ACKNOWLEDGEMENTS

So-called sole-authored books are seldom such. I depend heavily on many family members, friends and colleagues for their support and patience as well as their direct assistance. I take the blame for blemishes and blunders, of course, but if I can see anything clearly it is because I stand on the shoulders of others. Warm thanks to those who kindly and critically read drafts of this book: Colin Bennett, Andrew Clement, Chiara Fonio, Miriam Lyon, Midori Ogasawara, Chris Prince, Charles Raab, Priscilla Regan, Emily Smith, Valerie Steeves, Didier Bigo and Steve Anderson. Andrea Drugan and the readers for Polity Press also gave valuable direction. Some ideas from published articles found their way into this book, particularly 'Surveillance, Snowden and Big Data' in *Big Data & Society* 1.1 (2014) and 'The Snowden Stakes' in *Surveillance & Society* (2015). I am constantly grateful for the encouragement and help of Joan Sharpe and, especially, Emily Smith, as well as graduate students, post-docs and visiting scholars – this time, Marta Kanashiro – in the Surveillance Studies Centre at Queen's University, which is itself an affirming context. Our children and, now, grand-children, display a buoying interest in my work. And although this is not the only or best time or place for acknowledging Sue's steadfast support, consistently expressed for well over four decades, I cannot but mention her here. To miss her out would be to miss the most.

INTRODUCTION:

CITIZENFOUR ALERT!

For now, know that every border you cross, every purchase
you make, every call you dial, every cellphone tower you
pass, friend you keep, site you visit and subject line you
type is in the hands of a system whose reach is unlimited,
but whose safeguards are not.

Edward Snowden to Laura Poitras, 2013

The day after the Snowden story broke in *The Guardian*
newspaper in June 2013, I was reading the breathless reports
on a flight to Victoria, British Columbia, where I was sched-
uled to give a conference lecture on 'The Emerging Culture
of Surveillance'.[1] The mass media were clearly reeling from
the scope of the scoop: some astounding revelations – the
largest leaks ever[2] – about the activities of the highly secretive
National Security Agency (NSA) in the US. Many had suspected for some time that the sprawling NSA was responsible

for very widespread, rather intrusive but surreptitious surveillance of ordinary citizens.

But what we learned considerably exceeded those suspicions. Telephone and internet companies, we were stunned to learn, were sharing our personal data with security agencies regularly and frequently. Familiar names in the telecoms and internet world, such as Verizon and Microsoft, were implicated in the mass surveillance of ordinary citizens in the United States but also in many other countries around the world.

The main character, we soon discovered, was a quiet but confident 29-year-old first known to journalist Glenn Greenwald by the codename 'Cincinnatus' or to filmmaker Laura Poitras as 'Citizenfour', and now known to all as Edward Snowden. At the time, he had just engaged in high-level discussions in a Hong Kong hotel room with Poitras and Greenwald, to whom he handed countless documents for timed release. In the surreal drama, footage for the Oscar-winning film *Citizenfour* was already being shot. Over the next few days and weeks, large-scale damage-control was under way, from both government and corporations. But the secrets were already out.

Back in the hushed lecture hall at the University of Victoria, the chair of my lecture pointed out the amazing serendipity of the occasion, although she also noted that surveillance had already become a consistently prominent news feature, especially since the 2001 attacks on America known as 9/11. So I proceeded to give my talk as calmly as I could while the hot news of Snowden trended, politicians spoke wildly of 'traitors' and the certainty of their punishment, and journalists scurried to find experts to interview on the damaging disclosures.

Before going further, let me say how I understand 'surveillance', the key concept of this book. Although many think of surveillance primarily as something that police and intelligence agencies do, it is important to consider how their activities in fact very closely resemble what many other organizations – such as marketing companies – do as well. As a historian and sociologist I have to say that surveillance is a much more general activity; 'collecting information in order to manage or control' sums it up for many contexts.

More particularly, surveillance could be defined as any systematic and routine attention to personal details, whether specific or aggregate, for a defined purpose. That purpose, the intention of the surveillance practice, may be to protect, understand, care for, ensure entitlement, control, manage or influence individuals or groups. In this book, we are thinking mainly about surveillance involving human beings, although it may actually be the devices – such as cellphones – that are the bearers of the surveillance data. Many everyday technologies produce evidence about what we say and do and they are very much part of the surveillance process. This also means that how we use those devices affects how successful is the surveillance. The outcomes are never inevitable.

In my talk at the University of Victoria I pointed out that for a long time state surveillance has prompted 'Orwellian' thoughts and fears but that towards the close of the twentieth century people started pondering the possibility of a 'surveillance society' beyond 'government' monitoring. Indeed, by the start of the twenty-first, 'Big Brother' seemed to be employing loyalty cards and even Facebook to keep tabs on everyday life in the commercial sector.[3] But the point of the lecture was to stress that, as well as the surveillance state and surveillance society, we now have to take account of surveillance culture. Surveillance is not just practised *on* us, we participate *in* it. This is very recent.

Ironically, the surveillance culture came prominently into view simultaneously with the intensified security surveillance following 9/11 and the so-called war-on-terror. The irony lies in the fact that some of its main carriers – social media and hand-held devices – were promoted as technologies of freedom and fun. Few popular connections were made between Facebook friends and state snoops.[4] Yet the two have links and, even more ironically, the Snowden revelations show clearly that government surveillance carried out by the NSA and its equivalent agencies around the world depends heavily on data gleaned from Facebook posts, Twitter feeds, cloud services such as Google Docs and smartphones that record where we are by GPS.

In other words, in a surveillance culture we participate as never before in our own surveillance by willingly sharing our personal information in the online public domain. One imagines Orwell turning in his grave: have we all become Winston Smiths, loving Big Brother? That is one question we have to grapple with in this book.

Writing began not many months later, when my editor, Andrea Drugan, suggested I tackle the topic of surveillance after Snowden. She wanted me to put the revelations in a larger, longer context and to highlight the implications for social and political life, for ethics and for democracy. Of course, Edward Snowden has himself commented on some of these things, making frequent reference, for instance, to George Orwell.[5] As he said in December 2013, 'The types of collection in [Nineteen Eighty-Four] – microphones and video cameras, TVs that watch us – are nothing compared to what we have available today. We have sensors in our pockets that track us everywhere we go. Think about what this means for the privacy of the average person.'[6] But he did not stop there. Even in this, his first televised broadcast after taking refuge in a Moscow hotel, he said that his purpose was a democratic and participatory one: 'I wanted to give society a chance to determine if it should change itself.'

We now know a lot more about Snowden, his motives and his message, from a number of interviews and public appearances that he has made through complex electronic links. Weaving these into this present book will help us to see how he, a former NSA contractor-turned-whistleblower, understood the mass surveillance that he encountered on a daily basis. He hoped in vain that others would speak out, or even answer his questions. But Snowden's own stance has to be seen in context. As a young, tech-savvy participant in a digital world, he grew up using computers and social media. He observed from within the NSA the systematic sucking-up of personal information into a voracious vacuum by government agencies and their outsourced contractors. He, like many of us, *lives* technology's contradiction and so we have to hear his voice.

The Key Issues

Snowden's stance is controversial. Immediately following the first revelations he was branded both a traitor and a hero. Knowing all too well he could not assume the availability of legal protection for whistleblowers in the US climate, he chose self-imposed exile and was eventually given refuge in Russia. The massive concentration of media attention on Snowden as a 'squealer' and a 'spy' was not only a reflex of the search for sensational scoops. In part it relates to celebrity culture, where juicy details are tirelessly sought, but in part it was also a response to the government narrative that has insisted since 9/11 that only because of new heightened security measures and information collection are we ourselves safe from terrorist attack. 'Snowden has made us all more vulnerable' was a common cry, especially from security agency spokespersons. Indeed, the authorities went to some lengths to demonstrate their power and resolve, undoubtedly subjecting Snowden's personal data trail to some extraordinary searches in order to locate and punish him, as he had known they would.[7]

The *Surveillance after Snowden* title is intended to highlight the surveillance issues raised by Snowden, not to dwell on the personality, whereabouts, or motives of the man. Again, Snowden himself wants this, not publicity for himself. From the start, he planned to pass the documents to reliable and respected journalists who would determine the order in which the leaks would occur.[8] And in each public appearance since he has stressed his role merely as a go-between, a facilitator, someone who observed wrongdoing in public life and believed that others should know about it. So while the story as it broke would not exist without Snowden, it is surveillance, not Snowden, that should be the focus of our attention. At the same time, as we shall see, Snowden's own role and stance in the drama is significant.

Nor is this book about all the details of the 'revelations'. For one thing, the disclosures are disparate, across a range of practices and countries, and anyway they are as yet incomplete. For another, the revelations are publicly detailed and now archived in the Snowden Digital Surveillance Archive.[9] The revelations themselves do hold great interest for groups that question or oppose the kinds of state surveillance that have been shown to occur, on a far greater scale than imagined by most. This book tries to make sense of the Snowden documents by showing what is behind them and what responses are available.

Who knew that telephone and internet companies cooperated so freely, it seems, with government agencies or that specific target groups such as environmentalists were deemed to be as risky as 'terrorists'? The widening range of targets revealed by Snowden, along with the very broad channels of personal data collection, are crucial aspects of the revelations. No longer are such matters mere abstract speculation; they are now attached to solid evidence. Making such evidence publicly available is Snowden's achievement. Together, the revelations highlight some emerging trends in surveillance that are profoundly important. They deserve the most critical and urgent attention.

So what do Snowden's revelations about mass surveillance show? They offer extensive insights into the inner workings of the NSA and well beyond. Among other things they indicate that mass surveillance is carried out promiscuously on all kinds of people, without regard to conventional distinctions, such as 'US persons' and 'foreigners' – the latter including close allies. Who is particularly likely to be under such surveillance? The main explicit aim is to focus on terrorists but it has become increasingly clear that others, especially if they are protesters or they disagree with government policy, are potential targets.

Citizenfour refers to another NSA leaker who reports that there are now an astonishing 1.2 million Americans on the US government's watchlist of people under surveillance as a potential threat or as a suspect. So while some details of the Snowden revelations are tantalizingly patchy, for the most part the sheer volume of files and the range of areas to which they refer are nothing short of mind-boggling. And although the drip-feed disclosures began in June 2013, they continue to be released, with the result that any commentary is incomplete and partial.

Several major diplomatic events have been sparked by the revelations. Angela Merkel, Germany's Chancellor, and Dilma Rousseff, the Brazilian President, for example, were shocked to discover that their cellphone conversations had been monitored in August 2013.[10] Individual populations outside the US also reacted negatively on finding that the

NSA and its partners had been active in unexpected ways within their national territory. In Thailand, when an employee of the French-Dutch SIM card maker Gemalto sent some encrypted files, Britain's GCHQ and the NSA in the US took it as a signal that what he sent was valuable information. This was the start of an alleged 2010 digital break-in at Gemalto in the Netherlands, in which a GCHQ and NSA team hacked into the manufacturer's systems, using malware implants, and took encryption keys that allowed them to secretly monitor both voice calls and data. Gemalto produces more than 2 billion SIM cards each year, which are used by everyday names, AT&T, Verizon, Sprint and T-Mobile. The breach makes many millions of phone-users vulnerable.[11]

And in Canada it was disclosed that the NSA had set up shop in Ottawa in order to monitor the G8 summit and the G20 Toronto summit in June 2010.[12] In the UK, where the innocuous-sounding Government Communications Headquarters (GCHQ) carries out its security and intelligence business, users of YouTube and Facebook were shocked to learn that the Tempora program was being used to tap fibre-optic cables to create a buffer of searchable information. Snowden documents showed it had shared these techniques with the NSA – and the NSA 'loves this program', he says.[13] In these examples, it seems clear that, commensurate with its resources and computer-power, the NSA acts as the lead 'eye' of the 'Five Eyes' partners that date back to the Cold War – Australia, Canada, New Zealand, the UK and the US – leaving the smaller 'eyes' tasks such as testing and development.

Surveillance: Three Dimensions

Broadly speaking, at least three dimensions of surveillance practices became strikingly evident during 2013, as

Snowden's chosen journalists opened the taps to let the news flow. One, governments engage in mass surveillance on their own citizens – contradicting basic democratic practice. The NSA is the largest government agency, but its activities are mirrored in many other countries as well. Two, corporations share their 'own' data supplies with government, to mutual benefit: the corporations seek government contracts and the governments seek access to data. Internet companies in particular, knowingly or not, collude with government to provide personal data. Three, ordinary citizens also participate through their online interactions – especially in social media – and cellphone use. Without necessarily being aware of it, we all feed data to the NSA and its sister agencies, just by contacting others electronically.

These kinds of surveillance became more publicly evident, thanks to Snowden. However, they were not necessarily new. Several key surveillance trends[14] are augmented by the use of large-scale data-collection and analysis techniques. Let me mention just two here. One is that contemporary surveillance grows like mushrooms, and makes ordinary everyday lives increasingly transparent to large organizations. Every internet search, every email, every text, indeed, everywhere one goes with an electronic device like a phone, if there is a router or wifi network, one's presence will be recorded in the coffee shop, classroom or office – and each of these adds to the store of data collected and analysed by organizations, both public and private.

And that is to mention only those that are online. Shopping in the store, going to the bank, driving down the street, walking through the park, working in the office, hospital ward, factory, school or wherever, making a phone call also generates usable data for those organizations and for others who have access to such information. The corollary, however, is that organizations engaged in surveillance are increasingly invisible to those whose data are garnered

and used. How could we possibly follow all those data
trails to find out where our data go and who uses our data
for what? As we shall see, the apparent paradox of greater
citizen transparency alongside the reduced visibility of surveillance agencies deepens with the advent of so-called 'big
data', understood here as the linking and analysis of very
large datasets.[15]

A second surveillance trend is the spreading role of 'security' in daily life, which prompts the use of extended surveillance, from neighbourhoods and travel arrangements to large
sporting and entertainment events. The quest for 'national
security' breeds big data practices, particularly through
efforts to pre-empt security breaches by a form of anticipatory surveillance first described, somewhat vaguely, by the
US Department of Homeland Security as 'connecting the
dots'.[16] The well-meaning aim is to try to prevent crime and
violence before it occurs – *Minority Report* style [17] – but the
drive to do so tends to suck innocent bystanders into the
surveillance system in unconscionable numbers, with dire
results for human rights and civil liberties. Many innocent
people have been needlessly stopped – and worse – on borders
and at airports, for example, because officials have come too
quickly to the wrong conclusion. The drawn lines went to
the wrong dots.

Of course, the surveillance implications of big data
approaches, such as using metadata – data about the length,
origin and destination of an electronic communication, for
instance – are just one dimension of new ways of structuring
information in a digital age. The present task is not to
catalogue potentially beneficial aspects of big data but rather
to focus attention on what sorts of surveillance issues are
raised in new ways by this restructuring of information –
especially ones that prompt civil liberties or privacy
questions.

Big data, like surveillance itself, is a complex set of practices, hard to understand. In themselves, we may say that surveillance and big data have some very positive effects, but they never exist 'in themselves'. They are products of technological, economic and political systems whose underlying ways of engagement with the world they reflect. Surveillance and big data are not inherently 'good' or 'bad' – but they are never 'neutral' either. They have to be probed and assessed further.

This is not easy. Surveillance today is no longer small-scale or narrowly focused. Nor does it exist only in some specific settings. Indeed, it spills over easily from one context to another. Just like today's world in general, where little seems to settle for long enough to become established, surveillance has entered a liquid state.[18] It flows freely from department to department, between government and commerce, and is even engaged in by ordinary people as they get in on the game.

But just as the effects of surveillance seem all too close to home, actually doing something about it seems remote. We may be politically active on a local level, but the centres of power are far from local. And, does one blame intensified surveillance on the agency, such as the NSA, or the legislature that made many of their activities legal, or, for that matter, the electorate that voted for tough-on-terror administrations? From colossal data centres to global networks of state and corporate power, to complex relations between agencies and government, the surveillance-industrial complex seems out of reach.[19]

Yet part of this book's message is that action can be taken. We do not have to throw up our hands as if nothing can be done or shrug our shoulders as if mass surveillance is someone else's problem. Privacy is a well-established human right that can be defended and used against unwarranted and unwanted invasions and incursions that squeeze spaces for democracy, or against the creation of lists and categories of persons that prejudice civil liberties. Ethical, technical, educational, political, legal and everyday community work cries out to be done to eliminate harms and to oversee and regulate surveillance agencies.

Surveillance after Snowden

We now know about some components of contemporary surveillance in greater detail and depth as a result of the Snowden revelations. Many aspects of mass surveillance have been discussed by experts over the past couple of decades, but what Snowden provides, in spades, is evidence. That evidence now needs to be sifted and checked with what was already known, across a range of different spheres, commercial and governmental, technical, organizational and cultural. We try to understand what is happening today in an immensely important area – how personal information is handled, by whom, for what purposes and with what kinds of consequences, for which groups? Using signposts from history, sociology and ethics we also find lessons about politics and democracy.

Snowden's revelations show clearly and starkly how surveillance has ballooned in recent decades and how it has become increasingly unaccountable and less and less visible to ordinary people. Organizations today make our lives more and more transparent, while at the same time their own activities become more difficult to uncover. After all, most surveillance is invisible. But ordinary people are also involved as we interact routinely with digital devices and electronic modes of communication. How we all respond to Snowden will also be important for the outcome, for the future of our social and political relationships.

Snowden has helped to throw light in dark places so that many more people can see that surveillance today is, in a sense, out of control. Surveillance is in the news and on the public agenda in new ways since Snowden. We can see that surveillance is carried out by government and commercial agencies acting together, sometimes deliberately, sometimes unwillingly. Each also operates under the 'security' slogan, which also requires urgent unpacking and exposure. What is 'security'? Is mass surveillance the right way to achieve it? These are matters of practical, everyday concern as well as being politically volatile. This book tackles them in order to show just how far-reaching the impacts of surveillance-after-Snowden are and why this is something that touches all our lives in profound ways.

Roadmap

The chapters that follow explore the main dimensions of surveillance-after-Snowden. In chapter 1, some details of the documents that Snowden revealed are examined so that Snowden's work can be situated and understood in its variety. The underlying trends start to show through in ways that make sense of what he let leak. Chapter 2 goes straight to the question of how messages are intercepted and data gathered, through cellphones and the internet, and with what consequences. Big government and big business dominate these processes. But in chapter 3, the impact on ordinary people is once again evident. How do 'big data' approaches show up in the work of security and intelligence agencies? Why is the controversial term 'metadata' so important? We may think we have 'nothing to hide' but the use of metadata does nothing to help us sleep easily. Chapter 4 revisits the question of privacy – that now seems more precarious than ever – and suggests that human rights, democracy and politics itself may be threatened by what Snowden has disclosed. It also hints at hope for change. Chapter 5 turns to the way in which each of these issues is framed. 'Orwellian' approaches give us worst-case scenarios but a parallel way forward is to imagine a different kind of world. Not a non-digital or surveillance-free world, but one in which rights are respected and democratic participation encouraged.

It is just this kind of world that Snowden himself has been struggling for. And, two years after the initial document disclosures, major movement is occurring in the US as well as elsewhere. In June 2015, a dramatic debate in the Senate ended with the the most significant surveillance reforms since 1978; the USA Freedom Act was passed. Clearly, Snowden prompted the process that produced this outcome. Actually cutting back aspects of a surveillance program in this way is unprecedented, especially after the anti-terrorist expansion following 9/11. Is the tide turning? Much too early to tell. Snowden stresses how much more needs to be done, on many fronts, and how this is just a good start. In what follows, we shall learn why.

1

SNOWDEN STORM

Nineteen Eighty-Four is an important book but we should not bind ourselves to the limits of the author's imagination. Time has shown that the world is much more unpredictable and dangerous than that.

Edward Snowden, July 2014.

The solidly rectangular, fortress-like buildings of the NSA rise forbiddingly from Fort Meade, Maryland. So much is visible on the surface, but another 10 acres of buildings are underground. The dark-tinted glass-clad walls of the office tower reflect images of what looks like a medieval moat with the sprawling fields of parked cars as a kind of protective barrier surrounding it. For many years, the NSA has been shrouded in mystery, clearly super-scale in operation but also in its degree of secrecy. The joke was that NSA stood for 'No Such Agency'. Most commentators have been forced to speculate on what really goes on inside, aware only that its employees cannot speak of it and that its chain of accountability seems to disappear in the clouds.

Few dare to voice their concerns but when they do they risk being framed as paranoid traitors. William Binney, co-inventor of the NSA's ThinThread program that analysed internet and other communications data, worked for more than 30 years at the NSA. He had climbed to Technical Leader for Intelligence when he resigned in 2001, in protest against increased domestic surveillance after 9/11. Investigated but not prosecuted, he still had to deal with an armed police raid on his home in 2007 and with opposition to his business by the NSA. J. Kirk Wiebe, another ThinThread inventor, also blew the whistle on the NSA. Thomas Drake, a former senior executive at the NSA, whose first day on the job was 9/11, also broke silence about the wastefulness and illegality of the NSA's security-threat data-gathering Trail-blazer project – which superseded ThinThread – in 2006 and was prosecuted under the Espionage Act in 2010.

Against this backdrop the revelations about mass surveil-lance provided by Edward Snowden blew the NSA's cover as never before. NSA as 'Not Secret Anymore' was the new joke. The documents he disclosed offer extensive insights into the inner workings of that clandestine community. Among other things they indicate with stark clarity – as Binney, Drake and Wiebe had said before – that mass surveil-lance is carried out by government agencies on 'US persons'.

In the US, the impact of citizen surveillance hits hard. Not just suspected terrorists or criminals, but average American citizens are monitored. This staggering fact shows that the stakes include not only privacy but democracy itself. Surely, authoritarian regimes such as China, or former Latin Ameri-can dictatorships like Argentina, Brazil or Chile, subject their own citizens to surveillance, not democracies?[1] This deviation from democratic practice in the US is indeed serious, but it also draws attention to an underlying problem. Why should indiscriminate mass surveillance be considered acceptable anywhere? Surely the distinction between citizens and foreigners itself is invidious in this case?

Snowden's exploits expose the undermining of the rule of law, the lack of care about human rights and the loss of liberty for innocent individuals. At the same time, they indicate how elite power is enlarged, and how the views of ordinary citizens are overridden. Dissent is endangered. The revelations shine light on a hugely expensive and elaborate enterprise of sophisticated surveillance that seems to have abandoned the attempt to distinguish between foreigners and citizens and whose remit clearly extends well beyond anti-terrorism. And this is why trusted officials at the NSA, who believed in the intelligence work they performed, felt it was their moral duty to expose the expansion of surveillance far beyond what was necessary for national security.

This chapter starts by examining the different kinds of NSA surveillance revealed by Snowden, before commenting on Snowden's statement that because of surveillance the world is more unpredictable and dangerous than ever. We then look at what had been quietly developing for decades – the slow cooker of surveillance – and lastly at the sea change represented by post-9/11 pressures and predicaments.

Under the Iceberg Tip

Snowden handed 58,000 secret NSA documents to journalists for them to release in ways that would have maximum impact, a story that Glenn Greenwald and Laura Poitras have begun to tell. Sorting out the evidence of different surveillance techniques and practices is a massive task and the way that the media has latched on to certain stories does not necessarily reflect their comparative importance. Even to think in terms of earlier evidence of NSA 'warrantless wire-tapping' of the communications of US citizens provided by AT&T technician Mark Klein in 2006 and publicized by James Bamford in 2008[2] gives little clue about the magnitude of what Snowden uncovered. As Andrew Clement says, the 'warrantless wiretapping program was the tip of a much bigger iceberg, covering all forms of communications traffic and implicating most of the major telecommunications carriers across the US'.[3]

Let us look at some dimensions of the iceberg that lie beneath the surface, below its warrantless wiretapping tip. Like icebergs, formed when glaciers meet the ocean and break off to float freely, the NSA's activities are distinctively layered. Three main layers have been made visible by Snowden. The first is the interception of data-in-transit (see figure 1). These are the Upstream programs, including for example, Fairview, which is how the NSA gains access to the 55,000 miles of optical cables that lie between the US and other parts of the world (see figure 2). These cables carry internet data to many places – we learned early about Germany or Brazil[4] – where, with the cooperation of local telecoms companies, millions of citizens were surveilled. The NSA and its partners are part of a global mass surveillance system about which most people in the world had no idea and which has profound implications at many levels.

The second layer of NSA surveillance is its access to stored data. The Prism program is the best-known example, not least because it was featured in one of the first of Snowden's revelations. It is also a primary data-source. This is a data-mining program run by the NSA with help from the UK's GCHQ. Started in 2007, it taps directly into the servers of US internet companies AOL, Apple, Facebook, Google, Microsoft, PalTalk, Skype, Yahoo! and YouTube. It collects,

identifies, sorts and stores chatroom posts, emails, file trans-
fers, internet telephone calls, login/IDs, metadata, photos,
networking, stored data, videos and video conferencing – and

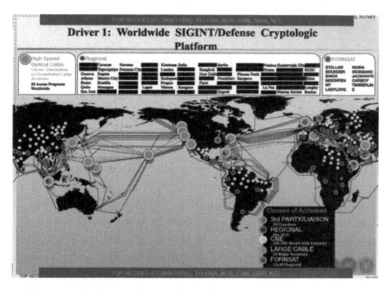

Figure 1 'Collect it all' signals intelligence (SIGINT) interception

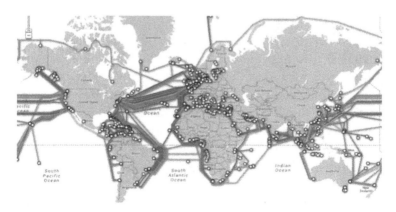

Figure 2 Submarine fibre-optic cabling (telegeography.com)

maybe more.[5] Although 'targeted' at foreigners, it also
touches American citizens 'inadvertently', 'incidentally' or
deliberately if an American is conversing with a foreign target
overseas. Again, no one guessed the audacity or the scope of
such data gathering, nor how well-known companies were
partnered with the NSA.

The third layer of the iceberg is the installing of spyware
on individual computers, a practice with the innocent-
sounding name of Computer Network Exploits (CNE). The
Gemalto SIM card case fits here. It is achieved by using
programs like Quantum Insert which, as well as capturing
data-in-transit, secretly injects malware into users' computers. In another European case, some technical employees at
Belgacom, a Belgian telecommunications company, pulled
up normal-looking LinkedIn pages that were in fact fake.
The lookalike pages contained invisible spyware that allowed
UK GCHQ operators to infiltrate Belgacom networks and
those of a subsidiary, BICS, that runs a so-called GRX router
system. From there, control could be obtained of cellphones
that use the router for making calls from abroad. Quantum
Insert is the system that enables these practices.[6] This means
that everyday devices may be infected with malware that is
constantly reporting back to spy agencies.

All this suggests that surveillance has in recent times been
ramped up to a much higher level than was imagined by
anyone before Snowden intervened. So many questions are
raised, it is baffling to decide where to begin. How can any
government expect to be trusted with their own citizens'
data? Who knows when their own telecoms provider is col-
luding with this surveillance? The systems described here are
highly secret, apparently unaccountable and growing by the
day. Perhaps the iceberg metaphor is useful for more than
the 'visible tip and submerged mass' and the 'distinct layers
of what is below the surface'? Another similarity may be that

these agencies seem to have floated free of the original entity
that produced them. They appear to work by their own logic
and rules.

Unpredictable and Dangerous

No wonder Snowden says that today's 'world is much more
unpredictable and dangerous' than Orwell could have
guessed. This is an urgent challenge from Snowden, not only
to upgrade our grasp of new technology, but also to place
any and all technological systems in their social, political-
economic and cultural context. The evidence suggests that
mass surveillance, developed with an apparently innocent
logic, ends up serving domestic purposes – finding 'bad
needles' such as environmentalists, Aboriginal protesters,
advocates against poverty, peace marchers or investigative
journalists in the data haystack – as well as external security.
And the use of metadata is not just the result of technological
potential and the exponential expansion of storage power,
but a tool used to manage risk in security industries and to
cluster consumers together for marketing in global neoliberal
contexts.[7]

Snowden says that more revelations are to come. Yet what
we do already know provides the basis for some serious
rethinking of assumptions about surveillance in the twenty-
first century. To take one prominent example, the very term
'surveillance' needs to be more carefully considered. What
now occurs seems to be without limit or discrimination.
Global mass surveillance is unprecedented in human history.
And what we now know about NSA practices raises questions
about the supposedly clear distinction between 'mass' and
'targeted' surveillance. Binney et al.'s ThinThread project
limited NSA surveillance by filtering out any domestic data,

leaving only foreign communications in the mix. However, the Trailblazer project that replaced it discarded this discretion even while it retained some of Binney's algorithms. The focus was widened to include Americans as well as foreigners, thus redefining what counts as foreign versus domestic collection. Trailblazer could be used to check telephone billing records and other personal information – 'metadata' – and this is also part of a trend towards collecting all kinds of data in order to build complex profiles of people and groups. This meant there was no longer anonymization to protect the data – and citizens of any country – from unwarranted prying.[8]

Not only did mass surveillance expand beyond targeted surveillance in the NSA at home in the US, but also in its intelligence counterparts around the world. It is increasingly evident in other surveillance domains as well, as we shall see. 'Mass' and 'targeted' surveillance have been thoroughly blurred. If data are sought on a mass basis, from wide swathes of a given population, with a view to identifying who might be a 'person of interest', the point at which 'mass' becomes 'targeted' surveillance is fuzzy at best. That identification is done using algorithms – the computer codes that guide how data are sorted – to create connections and to show correlations that may or may not add up to a solid lead.

A second concept to interrogate is 'privacy', regarded by the United Nations and in many countries as a basic right. Is this concept up to the task of saying in a nutshell what is lost with intensified surveillance? What exactly is included in 'personal data' or 'personally identifiable information'? This has been debated for many years. New technologies frequently throw up new challenges. Is someone's random Facebook photo featuring your image, or your vehicle licence plate, 'personal data'? We return to this is chapter 4.

When all kinds of apparently trivial data may become in a sense 'personal', information and the individual seem to part company. And as in many minds 'privacy' has to do primarily with the 'individual', old definitions are radically challenged. When speaking about metadata – such as your computer's IP address, the duration of your phone call, which friends were contacted – these are just the kinds of information that a private detective might seek: who spoke to whom, when, and for how long? Despite protestations to the contrary, it is hard to deny that such metadata is highly 'personal'.

This is not merely a 'technical' problem, as if such problems exist on their own. The gravitational pull of US security, commerce and law led to outcomes that are idiosyncratic in the US. The privacy and data protection regimes of many other countries are different from American ones, which further complicates the debate over how to treat 'metadata'. It also raises big questions about mass surveillance that operates not only within the US but between that country and its closer allies.

Things are constantly changing in the world of surveillance, as well as with surveillance critique. Snowden's commentary on Orwell provides a clear starting point. For many people, the Big Brother metaphor is still the one that fuels the imagination regarding mass surveillance. But Orwell's dystopian and cautionary tale needs a context. For Snowden, this is primarily a technological matter; 'quaint' microphones hidden in bushes and the telescreen that can observe us have given way to mobile webcams and network microphones in cellphones. Orwell cannot be blamed for not foreseeing new technological advances. But he did see surveillance partially as an outcome of a relentless rationality expressed in bureaucratic procedures.[9] This undoubtedly helps to explain why surveillance is in one sense self-augmenting.[10] But more is needed.

Can we 'go beyond' Orwell? In the twenty-first century, the logic of resource maximizing has helped to drive deeper into the administrative fabric the older bureaucratic impetus to surveillance. Any government that wishes to minimize risk, lower costs and allocate finite human resources will be tempted to use mass electronic monitoring. Recording and accounting occurs anyway so there is little extra cost in adding some invisible, unreported elements that can be piggybacked on the existing infrastructure. The downside is that, almost imperceptibly, lines are crossed and that self-augmenting logic actually creates a new situation. Terrorism suspects are joined by unrelated others caught in the surveillance web, including for example many engaged in fully legal democratic activities such as environmental protest.

Snowden rightly describes the world of post-Orwell surveillance as unpredictable and dangerous. Few saw it coming on such a scale and, unfortunately, their voices went unheeded or their fears were downplayed. Of course, Orwell himself aimed his invective at supposedly liberal democracies but his work has all too often been seen as depicting state socialist regimes such as the former Soviet Union. But the fact of mass surveillance in liberal democracy is exactly what drove Snowden to take action which was personally costly to shine a floodlight on what was going on inside the 'land of the free'. He had evidence that mass surveillance had been turned against those who blithely believe they really inhabit a free society.

Who Saw It Coming?

However huge the revelations are, little is completely 'new' about what Snowden brings to light. Granted, the scoop value for journalists of the Snowden disclosures lies in the substantial store of clear evidence pointing to the present and ongoing reality of mass surveillance. This is undoubtedly new. When the news first broke in *The Guardian* on 5 June 2013, several factors were startling. It was reported that Verizon, the telecoms giant, was required by the NSA to give information on all calls within the US and between the US and other countries between April and July that year. This meant secret domestic spying on an astounding scale was happening under President Obama.[11] The international media, legal and activist outcry against the realities of mass surveillance now revealed gave the impression that citizens were quite unaware and unprepared for what they now were hearing.

Understandably, there was consternation, anger and outrage, in a variety of contexts simultaneously. Companies were upset that their global market shares became volatile. Lawmakers were disturbed by the demonstration that they did not seem to understand their own laws. Media and legal communities, who thought that their communications were immune from government scrutiny, felt betrayed. Official oversight bodies felt that they had been co-opted by government. As for human rights and civil liberties groups, they berated governments and security agencies for apparently condoning quite illegal activities. Everyday citizens expressed their own discomfort and shock at the apparent brazen lies about the scale of data collection and the dawning realization that they – we – were ourselves targets. The shock waves were felt almost everywhere.

Surveillance was not really on the radar of most ordinary citizens. Many worried, rightly, about the assault on privacy, but all too often this is construed only as a personal – understood as individual – matter. It is, of course, but there is also much more to it. Surveillance also operates in ways that affect whole groups in the population – like people in poverty, or Muslim Germans, or North Africans in France. This process is often referred to as social sorting,[12] targeting primarily population groups before individuals. The main exception to the focus on individual privacy is among those whose concern is violations of communications privacy. This does, however, prompt weighty questions about trust. For such critical minority groups, privacy is always bundled together with civil liberties and human rights.

Since the news first broke, the popular and media debate over Snowden has focused all too frequently on state surveillance primarily as a threat to prominent individuals such as Chancellor Merkel in Germany and President Rousseff in Brazil – except where the challenge to a free and open internet has been recognized. Yet the evidence shows that arbitrary power is used against all citizens when mass surveillance is practised. As a number of advocates have argued for some time,[13] privacy is not only an individual matter. Surveillance and privacy can each be considered along a spectrum of relationships, from the person to the population. By definition, mass surveillance means that anyone and everyone can be caught in the surveillance net and the larger the scale of surveillance, the more likely it is that mistakes – such as misidentification and misinformation – will occur.

Despite earlier leaks and studies there seems to be little public understanding of surveillance as it is practised today. The astonished (and astonishing) media sound bite is 'who knew?'. Yet the sorts of techniques uncovered by Snowden are ones that have a long history, not only in the annals of intelligence gathering and national security agencies, but in other spheres from policing to public administration to consumer marketing. The US Church Committee hearings on the Central Intelligence Agency (CIA), Federal Bureau of Investigation (FBI) and NSA in the 1970s and the Canadian McDonald Commission are cases in point.[14] Each investigated allegations of illegal surveillance activities in state agencies. And, in addition to the judicial inquiries, other whistleblowers spoke out about mass surveillance long before Snowden. Anyone who cares about freedom, democracy and justice in the twenty-first century should be concerned about the rampant growth of government surveillance.[15] It is worth briefly reviewing that development and how things have changed.

Decades of Development

In the Europe and North America of the 1980s surveillance was discussed in terms of the state, the workplace, policing and, even at that time, the consumer realm – so-called 'direct marketing' grew rapidly from the late 1980s.[16] In each case, much interest focused on the ways that new computer and communication technologies would enhance surveillance capacities. Sociologist Gary Marx, for example, pointed to what he called the 'new surveillance' in policing, influenced deeply by technologies that sounded at the time like the science-fiction portrayals from J. G. Ballard's 'The watch-towers', through Philip K. Dick's *A Scanner Darkly*, to Ray Bradbury's *Fahrenheit 451*. As Marx said, 'Like the discovery of the atom or the unconscious, new control techniques surface bits of reality that were previously hidden or didn't contain informational clues. People are in a sense turned inside out, and what was previously invisible or meaningless is made visible and meaningful.'[17] When Marx saw what was being used to find personal details – video, audio, heat or light sensors and, tellingly, meanings given to behaviour 'judged relative to a predictive profile based on aggregate data' – he could also see red flashing lights of warning.

Marx's concerns about the 'computer as informer' extended to other contexts. As government, business and everyday workplaces became increasingly automated, so checking and

tracking individuals often meant installing devices such as
video cameras or using the computers themselves as a way of
following the trails of citizens, employees or consumers.
While Orwell provides some helpful clues to these processes,
based in a rationalizing bureaucracy, his contemporary
Aldous Huxley suggests the subtle ways in which surveillance
would expand during the later twentieth century. His 'negative utopia' *Brave New World* showed how personal identity
would be lost when the search for stability in a fast-paced
world dominated political and social life. The central motif
is controlling, or, rather, 'conditioning' the population.
Important clues lie here, as well as in Orwell.

Governments have for centuries found ways of registering,
counting and keeping tabs on citizens. Similarly, employers
have always been interested in increasing the performance
of their workers and finding ways of keeping discipline. In
the early twentieth century, so-called 'scientific management'
broke work tasks down into separate components and timed
each in order to increase production. Once computers
entered the workplace, this could be extended down to key-
stroke counting in order to speed the tasks and check on
'slackers'. And although customers like to think of themselves
as making 'free choices', since at least the mid-nineteenth
century corporations have assembled records to manage
them, too.[18]

By the 1990s, the term 'surveillance society' was in much
more general use, indicating how once-restricted surveillance
was spilling over into everyday life.[19] State surveillance per-
sisted but systemic surveillance of many kinds could now be
expected simply as a result of conducting one's daily affairs.
Increasingly, surveillance became visible through ubiquitous
cameras in public streets and shopping malls, the use of credit
cards and loyalty cards, and then through online interactions
that expanded after the development of the World Wide

Web in 1994 and the subsequent commercialization of the internet, from 1995.

During the 2000s, two decisive events occurred that would shape surveillance decisively. One was 9/11 in 2001, as well as the London bombings of 7/7 in 2005, along with the 2004 attack on the commuter rail network in Madrid. The aftermath of these attacks hugely boosted security-related surveillance by the state, at least in the global north. Interestingly, in light of the increasing connections between government agencies and business corporations, the activities of the US Department of Homeland Security (DHS), quickly formed in 2002, took some cues from 'customer relationship management' (CRM) in the marketing world in their quest for 'Total Information Awareness' (TIA)[20] of citizens.

The other event was the invention of Facebook in 2004 – not the first social network of its kind, but the most globally successful in propelling social media into the mainstream. Facebook facilitated new levels of consumer surveillance and social surveillance, now based on self-expressed preferences and tastes.[21] By President Obama's inauguration in 2009 the Department of Homeland Security had developed a Social Networking Monitoring Center to check for 'items of interest' on its citizens and abroad.[22] Social media and state surveillance seemed destined to form an alliance from the earliest days of Facebook. They used similar methods, and agencies such as the NSA would take advantage of just the kinds of data already being collected and analysed by social media companies.

The Snowden revelations are a wake-up call to citizens still unaware that the day of mass surveillance of ordinary citizens has already dawned. After 9/11 the 'national security' rationale for intensified surveillance[23] became prominent and with it the use of data analytics (now generally referred to as 'big data').[24] The TIA program depended on a very large-scale database using 'new algorithms for mining, combining and refining data'[25] that included cash machine use, credit card trails, internet cookies, medical files and social media sites – anything, indeed, that might produce interesting correlations that might indicate meaningful relationships between records. These, the Snowden files show, are included among the methods used by the NSA in its surveillance both domestic and foreign.

Without doubt, Snowden is right to raise issues of privacy, civil liberties – including freedom of expression, communication and assembly – and human rights in relation to the NSA and its related agencies around the world. But deeper questions are raised that challenge many conventional assumptions about today's societies, their actual forms of power, their politics and their democratic institutions and processes.[26]

To see this merely as a question of electronically enhanced bureaucratic power bearing down upon hapless citizens is misleading. Certainly, citizens are made vulnerable as never before. But it is also about how citizens engage with the everyday, in communication, interaction and exchange, much of which occurs using digital devices that leave recordable, searchable traces. It is also about a surveillance culture[27] in which an increasing proportion of the world's population lives and to which, for a number of reasons, many have become accustomed.

Following the Trends

What are the major trends in surveillance today? The documents released by Snowden give us a view from inside secretive agencies. But it is helpful to see these against the backdrop of some key issues of contemporary surveillance that have become increasingly evident in the past decade or so. One trend is obvious: surveillance is an exponential growth area. It has become a basic mode of organizational practice, across a range of bodies, public and private. Beyond this, several other significant trends may be identified.[28]

As mentioned earlier, security is becoming a key driver of greater surveillance, not only at the 'national' level but also in general types of policing, urban security and in workplaces, transit systems and schools.[29] But beyond this, we have to ask if the current high priority given to 'security' might be trumping politics itself.[30] This is explored in chapter 4 but the basic line of argument is that assuming national security is the top priority removes the possibility for debate and undermines the position of those who argue that other priorities – such as *human* security: feeling safe, having enough to live on – compete with the thing called 'national' security.

At the same time, this trend towards the 'national security driver' of surveillance growth must be seen alongside another, the intertwining – and in some respects integration – of public and private agencies. The governmental and the corporate have always worked closely together in modern times. But the idea that they inhabit essentially different spheres, with different mandates, is currently unravelling. In areas like security especially, there is a revolving door between company directorships and posts as high-ranking government officials.[31] This may in part be a result of the emergence of 'trusted communities', guild-like formations of people distinguished by holding the highest level of security clearance, in either a government agency or a business. As Snowden reveals, telephone companies such as Verizon and internet companies such as Microsoft work in tandem with state agencies such as the NSA, in ways that have yet to be fully understood.

Several other important trends also deserve mention. Mobile and location-based surveillance is expanding, which means that 'where-we-are-when' – or, more technically, the time-and-space coordinates of our lives – are increasingly monitored. Surveillance is more and more embedded in everyday environments such as buildings, vehicles and homes. Machines recognize individual owners and users through card-swiping or voice-activation.

The human body is itself the source of surveillance data, with DNA records, fingerprinting and facial recognition coming to be viewed as reliable means of identification and verification. Moreover, all these trends are rapidly being globalized, which is in itself a surveillance trend in its own right. As noted above, social surveillance via networking sites is rising, a topic we return to below. And in all this, it becomes steadily more difficult to know what exactly counts as 'personal data'. Licence plates, presence in group photos posted on social media, and of course metadata make definition difficult.

All this challenges anyone wanting to understand surveillance today, and any and all citizens of contemporary liberal democracies in general. There are, however, some more questions to ask. Above all, is talk of a 'post-Snowden world' justified? Is surveillance significantly different from what we thought, now that the Snowden documents are becoming available? At the end of the book we review this question, but here I set out some factors that signal a surveillance sea change. Needless to say, these are also areas about which we do not yet know enough. So these factors each indicate a new situation which itself limits our capacity to see it clearly.

Post-9/11: Surveillance Sea Change?

The apparent disregard of what we already know about surveillance produces a sense of surprise about Snowden, rather
than sober expectation. Equally, however, it has to be admitted that current social science research, investigative journal-
ism and political opinion have yet to catch up with some vital
surveillance developments. Why? Part of the problem is the
obscurity of high technology. Most of us do not understand
algorithms, digital infrastructures and statistics. Nor do we
really know enough about professional networks such as
those operating in the security-and-surveillance world. It is
a shadowy environment, frequently cloaked in secrecy.

As for social media practices, the sheer pace of change
makes this difficult to follow, as well as the fact that different
networking platforms exist in different parts of the world.
While in Western Europe and North America it might be
safe to assume that most know about Google, Facebook or
Twitter, this is manifestly not the case in huge countries like
China, where Wechat, used for chat and photo-sharing,
Weibo, which is like Twitter, and Renren, which is similar
to Facebook but declining in popularity, are the main platforms. Lastly, the terms used to describe the data cast a
further shadow over the realities of post-Snowden surveillance. As we saw earlier, 'personal information' is not what
we once thought and capturing such data, we are told, is not
surveillance.

There is no conspiracy here, just an analytic fog that has
to clear before the contours of each situation can be seen
more sharply. And while talk of conspiracy is probably mis-
placed, this is not to say that lack of clarity and technical
complexity are not used by some as a smokescreen. As the
mistiness clears, the post-Snowden sea change will be sharply

evident. The Snowden storm cannot be contained in a teacup. But its true turbulence will not be felt until the insulating blanket of fog has dissipated.

Seeing through Techno-Fog

The first issue – technical complexity and the limits of everyday language – is one that may be most dramatically seen in relation to cloud computing – fog again? – and the electronic transfer of data from place to place. The metaphor of the cloud originated in diagrams intended to demonstrate how information is moved around.[32] The impression given – and reinforced through cloud marketing – is that somehow data flit weightlessly through the ether when in fact the actual conduits are fibre-optic cables. There are very real-world geographical and material elements to the cloud that belie the benign, fluffy, floating image. Think 'castle' not 'cloud'.

That buildings, bunkers, cables and conduits are still the stuff of surveillance is crucial to power configurations. Part of this has to do with the leading role of the US, through the NSA. While the 'cloud' may sound immaterial, in fact these electronic conduits include some very solidly material and heavily energy-consuming data centres, through which data travels. Cables criss-cross the US and also lie on the ocean floor, connecting continents (see figure 2 earlier). But because of the NSA's historic commitment to intelligence gathering, international data are frequently routed through the US and thus through data centres in places like New York, Seattle and Chicago, susceptible to NSA interception.[33]

NSA programs, often through the UK GCHQ, use such cables for collection of data – for instance, Upstream, Quantuminsert, and there are also commercial versions of such hacking programs[34] – and for interception – Tempora. Interceptors are placed strategically along the cable routes, a practice undertaken by many countries, and through security agreements with private companies such as Global Crossing much of the world's fibre-optic cable is accessible to the US (see figure 3).[35] More targeted NSA surveillance occurs using programs like XKeyscore, which is linked to the Prism program. XKeyscore is a system for searching and analysing internet data that the NSA collects daily, and it also stores material in data caches spread around the world in specific locations (see figure 4).[36] Prism, in turn, is a data-mining program that depends largely on consumer data obtained from internet companies through social media and cloud platforms.[37]

It is worth stressing again that while the NSA is the largest and best-funded agency engaged internationally in intelligence gathering, mention of the UK's GCHQ is a reminder that these activities are undertaken in partnership with allies.

Figure 3 Fairview 'Upstream' cities

Figure 4 Where is X-KEYSCORE?

And in some cases the partners are also engaged in international spying. In January 2015, for example, it was revealed that the Canadian Communications Security Establishment (CSE or CSEC) uses a system mischievously called 'Levitation' to tap into internet cables to analyse up to 15 million downloads from websites used to share photos, videos, music and other files.[38] It operates in the Middle East, North Africa and Europe as well as North America, often bypassing the companies, tapping the cables through a source codenamed 'Atomic Banjo'. Despite the ban on targeting Canadians, in one named instance, IP addresses trace back to a Montreal server appearing on a list of suspicious downloads.

Identifying the Watchers

The second murky issue is this – it is hard to pin down exactly who is conducting surveillance. Although the term 'state' surveillance is common in everyday speech, those who stand in for 'state' employees are many and varied (and this follows from the point above about the blurring between public and private sectors). Snowden's own position before his departure with the documents illustrates this. He worked for Booz Allen Hamilton, a management consulting firm for technology and security services, whose expertise was subcontracted to the NSA.

The attraction of outsourcing includes the light regulations that apply to companies in the US, giving a fairly free hand to operators and, from a government perspective, the ability to distance oneself should operations be uncovered or go wrong. French security researcher Didier Bigo[39] has for some time drawn attention to the ways in which 'security professionals' now form an international network, operating in different countries but with extensive cooperation. These are intelligence agents, technical experts, police (both public and private), advisers and others whose immediate genesis lies in post-9/11 international anti-terrorism cooperation. Today, however, their activities have expanded into a network of considerable influence.

Importantly, older distinctions break down as this network of 'unease managers' – as Bigo calls them – develops. They connect public and private agencies, internal and external security, national and international interests, and so on. This development grows alongside the digitization of security and surveillance such that 'national' security is no longer 'national' in 'its acquisition or even analysis, of data...' which helps to blur 'the lines of what is national as well as the boundaries between law enforcement and intelligence'.[40]

This issue is related to at least two factors. One is that today's large communications corporations are nearly all global and that this meshes with the stated imperative for post-9/11 surveillance to be globally coordinated. The other, already mentioned above, is the uncertainty of who actually carries out surveillance, although the further point here is that a loose affiliation of professional organizations can be identified. They work together, learning from each other and developing their own protocols, rationales and surveillance practices.

As the examples from the US show, similar surveillance practices occur across the board, whether in the DHS, CIA, FBI, NSA or, for that matter, in Australia's Defence Signals Directorate (DSD), Canada's CSE, New Zealand's Government Communications Security Bureau (GCSB), the UK's GCHQ and agencies in other allied countries. These 'acronym' policing and intelligence organizations also rely on similar subcontracting organizations that display lookalike technical, statistical and political-economic activities.[41] Both policing and intelligence agencies have strong military connections that also influence their practices. The traffic is two-way: information handling is crucial to each, so that domestic policing becomes more data-heavy[42] and also echoes military methods.[43]

In all cases it is also clear that such organizations do not just react to perceived threats to national security or to criminal acts. They actively construct the target populations and refine the rationales for so doing. This is where the commercial connections with technology corporations also become centrally significant, in conjunction with government actors. Policy influences and is influenced by the corporate and technical approaches and practices. At an organizational and network level, then, relationships are manifold and complex.

The Human Connections

The connections with individuals is a third question for which we have insufficient answers. Internet and cellphone users clearly play a role in 'post-Snowden' surveillance but how does this work? What are the tissues connecting agencies, tech companies and target populations? It is important to recall that social media are, historically speaking, a very recent twenty-first century phenomenon. Yet they have grown at an astonishing speed and with amazing global reach that they are now one of the dominant aspects of internet use. While there is significant social research in this area,[44] serious study on how social media users operate in relation to practices and concepts of surveillance and privacy is still very much in its infancy. It is a vital research priority.[45]

At face value – and above all to generations not 'raised digital' – it seems strange that social media users would freely permit personal details to be widely and promiscuously circulated online. After all, such constant posting of identifiable material makes users vulnerable to intense surveillance both by the corporations that seek their data for marketing purposes and by policing and intelligence agencies. Such willing compliance would surely have puzzled and bothered Orwell, attuned as he was to the use of new technologies to obtain popular subservience to the state, but maybe not so much Huxley, who would have put it down to their successful conditioning.

In many ways today's situation is decidedly post-Orwellian. Not merely have the technologies of surveillance been hugely upgraded, but surveillance practices are also common to all organizations; they all have surveillance 'regimes'.[46] And beyond these organizations themselves, there is a more general surveillance culture in which all who use electronic media participate. In such a culture, surveillance is not only a form of entertainment but also something encountered in everyday life and in which many knowingly and actively engage themselves. It may contain apparent paradoxes – for instance, evidence from Austrian social media users shows high levels of concern and criticism about online surveillance through the platforms but also a significant lack of knowledge of how surveillance actually works and how their data are used – but they still see these media as basic to their lives.[47]

The age of users is also a significant factor in its own right. Before social media arrived, those already online expected, and were apparently comfortable with, acts of watching, recording, feedback and sharing. This fits particularly well with the life-stage of young people, but online practices tend to alter as such groups get older. Social media users are now the most intensively surveilled groups in the world, and many of them paradoxically also live in democratic societies. Global events and everyday global contact help to 'condition' them, to inure them to the surveillance that promises to keep them safe, protect their communities and permit them to parade their preferences. 'Surveillance' is simply not the word that they would use to describe the situation. It is merely the way the internet works, the conditions of current modernity. But it does not have to work the way it does at present.

So, what long-term impact will the Snowden revelations and their aftermath have in informing and – dare one hope – reorienting some practices of social media users? Finding out involves careful analysis of how users themselves perceive the situations in which they find themselves and the practices they pursue online. After all, no internet users are simply conditioned or controlled in the sense that they have no choice or no capacity for reflexive thought.

Weasel Words, Cryptic Concepts

Within today's surveillance systems, non-personal data are used to assemble identifiable profiles. Scraps of information are combined in new ways to create composite digital identities. What do I mean? Well, as Colin Bennett says, 'information available about us online cannot be split into two neat categories, some of it personal and some of it non-personal'.[48] We can be identified by all sorts of items that do not at first sight appear to be personal. Your vehicle licence plate or the IP address of your computer are good examples. Google says that the IP address identifies only the machine, which can of course be shared. Yet in many cases the IP address can reliably be connected with an identifiable individual and therefore with their browsing habits, blog posts or social media interactions.

This problem reveals a rift between security and intelligence agencies plus corporations on the one hand, and on the other, organizations committed to maintaining privacy and data protection. In Canada, for instance, the kinds of metadata – discussed in chapter 3 – collected by government agencies have been dismissed in official pronouncements as not pertaining to personal data. No, we are told, metadata is to the internet what a phone book is to telephone subscribers. Just facts that are publicly available, names, addresses and of course, the telephone number. But they are quite different. The phone book has names, addresses and phone numbers. The subscriber data for access to the internet contains many identifiers – readers may recognize IP (Internet Protocol), MAC (media access control) and SIM (subscriber identity module), but there are several others – and in any case the internet is used in many other ways than a telephone. We literally live online, engaging in many work, educational, political or professional tasks, which makes our online interactions very revealing. As Bennett says, we are easily identifiable even if we are not identified.

The problem for the post-Snowden world is that many security and intelligence agencies insist that the mere routine capture of data, without later intervention, is not surveillance. This despite the fact that their standard stated aim is

to trace terrorists before they act. So somehow the surveillance ceases to be such while the data caches are collected
and only becomes surveillance again at a later point in the
process. The complexities multiply.

The agencies concerned have sought personal data for
their investigations for decades. Officially, they were limited
by law in many countries, including the US. But once constant online monitoring began on the internet and expanded
with social media, security agencies simply sought access to
the data available there. The issue goes beyond privacy,
tightly defined, to questions of power. The struggle to define
personal information is intensifying in the post-Snowden era.

What Snowden has revealed raises basic questions about
the surveillance of everyday life today – just because such life
is now lived, in many parts of the world, online. Once, 'cyberspace' was conceived of as a sort of separate realm – a virtual
space. Now it is increasingly clear – as many ordinary users
now seem aware – that this was a mistake. Cyberspace is not
'apart' from the real world. Such views could produce a
certain irresponsibility among users – still seen in seemingly
thoughtless posts and tweets – along with a dangerous depo-
liticizing of what governments may do online. More recently,
however, there are some signs that expectations of online
respect, reciprocity, the means of recourse and the rule of
law are beginning to mirror those offline. The internet may
sometimes distract from aspects of the 'real world', however
that term is understood. But it cannot be seen as a separate
realm. Mass surveillance shows how 'online' and 'offline'
worlds are deeply connected.

2

WORLD WATCHING

Global mass surveillance is occurring...not just in the US. It is important to remember that this is a global issue.

Edward Snowden, March 2014

A cyber-attack on Sony Pictures in January 2015 was attributed to the North Korean state but it turned out that the NSA had planted malware that enabled this accusation to be made. From 2010 the NSA punctured Chinese networks connecting North Korea with the outside world, made use of Malaysian connections with North Korean hackers and, with help from South Korea and other NSA partners, penetrated what is one of the strongest digital fortresses in the world. The malware could keep track of many computers used by North Korean hackers, organized by the North Korean intelligence service.[1] It seems hard to find a place in the world where the NSA is not actively present.

The early shock value of the Snowden revelations was that security agencies such as the NSA spy on their own citizens. But the extent of global surveillance now laid bare is also astonishing. Marshall McLuhan said in 1970 that 'World War III is a guerrilla information war with no division between military and civilian participation' and this is exactly what spies seem to prepare for today.[2] Such global surveillance activity is basic to today's cyber-conflicts. While events in North Korea, facilitated by contacts in Malaysia and electronic connections in China, seem rather remote from many in Europe and North America, the NSA's global activities often touch on more mundane personal information.

The NSA has for years logged details of virtually every American phone call and from time to time has recorded details about email correspondence, too. If anyone contacted someone connected with someone else who may have corresponded with a terrorist suspect in another country, the NSA claims from the Foreign Intelligence Surveillance Court (FISC) the right to look at the contents of those emails. This 'right' is broadly interpreted, suggests Snowden, in this case to include 'US persons'. But the same NSA, and its partners in other countries, run similar programs around the world, which means that wherever it is used, the internet – not to mention telephone systems – are susceptible to state security interference and interception.

So when Snowden says that 'global mass surveillance' is occurring, he does not exaggerate. Such a system has never been developed before and although some may have suspected it and others wrote sci-fi nightmares about it, the recent revelations indicate that it really happens. Of course, it cannot mean that everything is actually under observation all the time. But it does mean that one agency, the NSA, and its partners and allies, along with collaborating corporations in many countries, have the capacity to monitor at will individuals and groups, organizations and governments using technologies that have been quietly developed over decades. The spy network is vast, scarcely visible, and very powerful. 'World watching' is not hyperbole.

Thus the questions raised by Snowden's revelations touch almost everyone's life. It may be that the NSA's 'interpretation' of the rules governing it is too broad, or that in fact some of the NSA's – and other agencies' – activities are simply illegal. Equally, it may be a matter of how the law is differently interpreted within and outside the agencies. But the revelations really show that the internet is not what many imagine it to be and that online privacy – including and especially from state agencies – can never be assumed.

Who else is involved? Well, internet companies have also been exposed, sometimes embarrassingly – although they often had little choice – as being implicated in the interception and data capture. They too have been obliged to respond, sometimes trying to distance themselves from the implications of the leaks, sometimes promising to encrypt users' communications to protect them in 'the cloud'. Google was one of the first corporations to make such assurances, in August 2013, encrypting all data warehoused in its Cloud storage service by default.[3] Thus, business interests were also profoundly challenged by Snowden's revelations.

Today the internet is bound up with surveillance at many levels and consequently deserves special attention. There is a sense in which the internet is where people live and at the same time it is an inherently surveillant habitat. Information and the internet are major features of today's world in our everyday lives and have a central place in the corridors of power. As journalist Glenn Greenwald comments, 'Internet freedom – the ability to use the network without institutional constraints, social or state control, and pervasive fear – is central to the fulfillment of [its] promise. Converting the internet into a system of surveillance thus guts it of its core potential.'[4] For him and many others, the Snowden revelations raise the future of the internet as a key issue.

Stepping back for a moment, we should recall that modern societies are all dependent on information and communications. Our reliance on the internet is simply the latest and largest example of this, although the internet is unprecedented in its scope and reach. Modern societies have always been 'information societies' – and therefore 'surveillance societies'.[5] Why? Well, the collecting and organizing of information on populations is a key part of the bureaucratic management of the nation-state as it has developed over the past 200 years. This is seen in registries for birth, marriage and death, in the census, driving licences, social insurance numbers, passports and the like, each of which involves forms of surveillance.

Now, information and its central channels have become an unprecedented arena of political struggle. What surveillance data government holds on ordinary citizens and how far citizens may know about government information are contentious issues. The fact that corporate and consumer information also flows in parallel and sometimes converging ways simply complicates things further. Thus to understand surveillance one must examine these storage containers and conduits of information, as well as develop a sense of appropriate practice and policy. In the twenty-first century the internet and surveillance are deeply intertwined; like ivy or vines growing on trees they depend on each other.

This chapter offers some essential background to today's debates over online surveillance. We begin by considering the high hopes and the recalcitrant realities with which the internet began: it was the product of both Cold War rhetoric and the democratic dreams of some computer enthusiasts. This shows how information and power are tightly connected today. Certainly this is demonstrated in the mind of John Poindexter who was behind the creation of the 'Total Information Awareness' program after 9/11 that information was the source of superior power – *scientia est potentia* (knowledge is power) was inscribed in its logo.[6]

Secondly, we shall see how the surveillance of communications has become a key source of data and how the way the internet currently operates facilitates this. Intercepting communications has been a central task of intelligence gathering for centuries but as Snowden shows, the cables and conduits of the internet – now often, misleadingly, referred to as the cloud – make possible mass surveillance as never before. Thirdly, we consider the global dimensions of the NSA's activities, affecting not only the US but its close associates in the Five Eyes, its allies such as Germany, Brazil, Israel and Japan, and its avowed enemies such as Russia or Iran. We conclude the chapter by exploring how the internet is thus a key area of struggle: free democratic communication versus consolidated information power.

Dreaming the Internet

The use of the internet for surveillance is not new but its scope has never been greater. For many, such as Greenwald and Snowden himself, this is a great betrayal of the initial wave of optimism about its democratic potential with which the internet was born. The hoped-for human benefit predated the commercialization of the internet but versions of it were also woven into many corporate aspirations in Silicon Valley and elsewhere from the 1990s onwards.

Back in the 1980s, some popular and visionary writers such as Ithiel de Sola Pool[7] foresaw the development of what we now call the internet, arguing that it was a key carrier of technological freedom. He insisted, however, that free speech would become a vital issue. How regulation and access were organized would determine whether or not the new communications would enhance democracy as the political platform and the printing press had done before. But he still stressed the 'freedom' idea. The Snowden revelations provide evidence to doubt such optimism.

A brief history of the internet gives some perspective. The growth of computer-and-communications, once referred to together as 'information technology' (IT), has been phenomenal. It is easier for me, as someone who has lived through the changes, to see this than it is for some of those who have 'grown up digital'. I was born just after the first transistor was invented (in 1947) and these semiconductor devices for amplifying and switching electronic signals were crucial to the early development of modern electronics. I recall proudly building my own transistor radio in my early teens.

In 1957, the first earth satellite was launched by the then Soviet Union, enabled by lightweight and compressed electronics, which stoked American Cold War fears of Soviet military dominance in space. This prompted an urgent search for light, tiny electronic components, and after the invention of the silicon chip in 1978 transistors themselves were miniaturized and built-into integrated circuits. Circuits were actually printed into wafer-thin silicon that eliminated the need for soldered wires and separate components.

Significantly, the Cold War also had an impact in the structure of ARPANET, the military predecessor of what eventually became the internet. The distributed and decentralized 'packet-switching'[8] between computer nodes was chosen to withstand a Soviet attack. Designers sought a system that was not dependent on any one node. Data would divert around any hub that was disabled or offline. The same fear-generated protocols were reproduced in the internet from the beginning. That attack anxiety is part of its very make-up.

The silicon chip that enabled all this was a vital building block for both computing and communications. It made possible the shift to the exponential growth of computing power *and* the capacity for computers to 'speak' to each other in networks. Sometimes, this was almost literally 'speaking'. When I first taught an IT-enabled distance learning course with the UK's Open University in the mid-1980s, the modem was an 'acoustic coupler' that converted electrical signals into sound when the telephone handset was plugged into a double rubber socket and they were then converted back into electric signals to enable the data to travel.

Over a decade or two, the size and cost of components fell rapidly, just as the power of IT rose dramatically. These heady days in the last part of the twentieth century were referred to as the 'information revolution'[9] and hopes were high that the military and intelligence origins of these apparently world-transforming technologies could be overtaken by new and desirable democratic and developmental purposes. It did not happen quite like that.

Personal computers were widely distributed in the global north from the 1980s and in the 1990s their connection through the internet became a reality, especially after the 1994 invention of the World Wide Web. This spawned many web-based industries and also the 'dot.com' boom and bust of the later 1990s. Alongside this, many other digital devices were taking shape, such as digital cameras, cellphones and games – all of which would very quickly be linkable with each other through the parallel growth of networks, the best known of which was the 'public' internet. I place 'public' in quote marks because, although the internet did help to democratize many communications, to the dismay of many its commercialization in the 1990s changed its character permanently.

Those digital devices were soon fully integrated with the internet, enabled by common technical systems. Digital cultures[10] emerge around each device and often around the whole cluster of photo-, audio- and text-sharing. They are usually characterized more by humdrum than hyped features. After all, we are surrounded by more things than ever – there is no 'paperless society' – and they change constantly. The movement is liquid. Mobile telephony is probably the most significant for the simple reason that it offers the chance to combine different platforms and applications – including internet access – in one device. From a surveillance point of view, the cellphone is also profoundly useful, not least because it generates much metadata – so significant to the Snowden revelations – including not only the identity of the caller but, crucially, the time, place and duration of contact.[11]

In the first decade of the 2000s cloud computing and the user-generated content of social media platforms appeared, and in the 2010s ubiquitous and pervasive computing became more evident.[12] But the apparent Silicon Valley successes were not that secure. For instance, the web-based companies that survived the disastrous crashes of the late 1990s were still searching for a more solid future. Many found it in the aftermath of 9/11 as they offered their services in the anti-terrorism cause.[13] It was thus no surprise when the Department of Homeland Security was shown (in 2011) to be checking through social media posts and email communications in search of potential terror suspects, using numerous keywords including 'pork' and 'cloud'.[14] After 9/11 it was mainly the DHS that found itself in the critical spotlight and it was not until Snowden's breathtaking document seizure that attention turned decisively to the NSA.

The term often used by aficionados from the period of early internet excitement was 'cyberspace' and this is a telling term. The idea, coined by William Gibson in 'Burning Chrome' (1982),[15] originates in the 'cybernetics' of the 1950s, which was the study of regulative systems and feedback loops in communications. The concept, as conceived by Norbert Wiener in 1948, focused on the study of control in communication systems, and originates in the Greek word *kubernetes*, for 'steersman' or, more generally, governor. Cybernetics is used in many contexts, but especially in relation to computer systems, and always with the aim of improving effective organization and management. This was certainly true of the use of the term 'cyberspace' in the context of control over the internet.

The story is one of both paradox and irony, tied inextricably to the Cold War and the eventually contrasting trajectories of Soviet and American cybernetics.[16] Norbert Wiener himself worried about the possible consequences for human societies of cybernetics and 'automatic machines', seeing in them both 'threat and promise'.[17] He was also scathing about the capacity of the 'invisible hand' of the market in US capitalism to bring about improved conditions for all, arguing that no cybernetic homeostasis was ever likely in the modern world of boom and bust, of revolution and dictatorship.

Opposed to the idea of the profit motive as a filter for information control, Wiener would turn in his grave to see today's giant companies, like Google, holding the data that the NSA wants. He used cybernetic theory to argue against controlling the means of communication – which he believed both Joe McCarthy did in pursuing 'communists' in the US and Stalin did in the Soviet Union. Like others,[18] he foresaw how easy it would be for even democratic governments to resort to effective manipulation. Eventually, in a final irony, Wiener's pacifist opposition to the bombing of Hiroshima put him under surveillance by the FBI.[19]

In a word, the internet was an ambiguous invention from the outset. It had obvious democratic potential – for instance, offering a voice to others who might not be heard – but as its main developers opted for a very technical vision of how it would operate, it is little surprise that the outcome was far from utopian. Moreover, as military and control designs were evident from the start, in its later development it has also served to connect diverse devices that also had strong surveilling and controlling tendencies.

For example, many of today's popular digital machines are characterized by their ability to record their own use. This certainly allows their 'cybernetic' use in providing feedback loops that help Amazon.com 'know' what products we're likely to enjoy, but it also lends a surveillant dimension to every cellphone. This is because the same handy features that can guide you through an unfamiliar part of the city may also readily 'report back' on your whereabouts to policing or intelligence agencies that might wish to track you.

What happened to those utopian dreams of the information revolution pundits of the 1980s? They had correctly noted the liberating and democratizing possibilities offered by the new technologies. But they did not pay enough attention to the already existing economic and political factors that together were influencing the development of information technologies – not to mention the tremendously strong and resilient cultural belief in the power of Technology.[20] Taken together, these led to a failure to note that the new technologies might be seen as 'solutions' despite evidence that they did not work quite – or at all – as promoted.

Snowden's revelations came like a cold shower. Right on the heels of the news about the NSA's access to Verizon telephone subscriber data came the disclosures about Prism, directly implicating major internet companies. Urgent exchanges occurred, some of which seemed to involve some puzzlement on the part of the companies. Yes, they had parted with some data but the revelations seemed to suggest

that far greater quantities were involved than they had themselves authorized. As it transpired, beyond the access authorized by the Foreign Intelligence Surveillance Act (FISA) to
data held by internet companies, the NSA had also found
ways to intercept the data flow upstream, by methods such
as Muscular system, developed by the NSA along with Five
Eyes partner, the UK government's GCHQ.[21]

Snowden's findings shine a spotlight on an issue of which
internet companies had been all too aware for some years.
Companies such as Google, Yahoo! and Twitter said they had
struggled to hold off government attempts, through the FISA
court, to oblige them to hand over customer data. The fact
of security clearance compartments does not help either.
Security experts within a company often work in a semi-
sealed, government-oriented pocket and are normally under
a gag order even within the company. CEOs and spokespersons may not know what goes on in that layer. To their credit,
the companies seemed to have tried to ward off government
efforts to obtain data but the combination of government
power and the significant fact that the companies also have
government contracts compromises the struggle somewhat.
Prism focused the fight, but the secrecy surrounding the
NSA has made it very difficult to know exactly what is happening. They are fighting in a fog. Part of the mistiness has
to do with how information is understood.

Information Is Power

What is information? Like all such concepts, its definition is
contested. How did it emerge in its modern form and how
has it come to dominate the ways in which surveillance
occurs? Answering that question helps us towards a definition. From the 1880s, steam power then electricity needed

innovations in communication and control to help coordinate processes. This was where modern information became increasingly important. Similar trends were seen in railway timetables, scientific management in factories and government bureaucracies. Most generally, information is communication or reception of knowledge or intelligence.

Before the Second World War, information was what you asked a telephone operator for, meaning a number. Or it was a dinner recipe or fire route instructions. The high-level Anglo-American Macey Conferences discussed information theory in the 1950s. At those meetings, what could now be seen as a fatal distinction was made between different understandings of information.

Claude Shannon argued, in his mathematical theory of communication, that the content of messages – the 'semantic' aspect – is irrelevant to the engineering issue of storage and transmission. As we shall see in the following chapter, talk of metadata follows the same logic.[22] The context of disclosing and receiving messages is not seen as relevant. Metadata is a technical matter; content has no connection with it. Privacy relates to content, therefore collecting metadata is not surveillance. Or so some surveillance agency spokespersons say.[23] In fact, fully disentangling metadata and content is impossible today.

Until the 1970s 'information' was still not a widely, or popularly, discussed matter, although security organizations were undoubtedly aware of its importance from the outset. When in the 1970s the idea that a society might experience an 'information revolution' was proposed, the two understandings of information were obscured but still present.[24] The practical – and consequential – outcome of the dual definition of information would not become fully evident until the debate over Snowden.

In the mid-1990s, *The Information Age* by the sociologist Manuel Castells[25] demonstrated how information had risen to prominence in relation to the diffusion of new electronic technologies and had become basic to economic, political and social life in the modern world. He spoke of an 'informational mode of development' that was flexible, pervasive, integrated and reflexive. Commercial competitiveness now depended on firms being able to generate and process information on an increasingly real-time and global basis, especially through global cities like New York, London, Tokyo, Shanghai, Hong Kong and Singapore. Interestingly, Castells also went on to observe that the commercializing of the internet was the 'key moment' for increased online surveillance.[26]

When so-called 'user-generated content' became the defining trait of Web 2.0, Castells referred to the emerging phenomenon as 'mass self-communication'.[27] By his own logic, this also spells surveillance. The network society, described in the first volume of *The Information* Age, in which all aspects of social, economic and political arrangements are affected by their reliance on the new technologies – is equally the surveillance society. This means that tendencies towards monopolies of influence and power are fostered by the very same technologies that also encourage the belief that free speech is available on the internet.

As Castells stresses, there is a built-in tension between the 'net' and the 'self'. And while earlier technologies may have emphasized their power over time – print media hold a long-term influence – or space – modern communications from the telegraph onwards supported globalizing trends, including colonialism – the internet has a role in each.[28] However, the internet pulls time and

space together by facilitating new forms of control that
squeeze social relations into new technically shaped moulds
while still trying to hold on to monopolies in the public
arena.[29]

No wonder, then, that control over information has
become such a crucial issue for governments, corporations
and the public in the twenty-first century. Hacktivism, that
uses computer systems for protest and to promote political
ends, emerged as a response, and names such as Wikileaks
and Anonymous are synonymous with controversies over
who owns what information and what should not remain
veiled in secrecy.

Julian Assange, the founder of Wikileaks, has been deliberately leaking secret documents about subjects such as
American military missions and life at the notorious Guan-
tanamo Bay prison camp, since 2006. He and his associate
Sarah Harrison were each involved in Snowden's search for
a safe haven after the June 2013 revelations began. Another
thorn in the flesh of government, Anonymous, is increasingly
known for its opposition to surveillance and political corrup-
tion.[30] Both organizations specialize in wresting information-
power from governments and corporations and opening it up
to ordinary people.

Given the growing secrecy-by-default in many organizations, and especially government agencies, the emergence of
such hacktivism and of open data groups is a logical response.
Even transparency has limits, however. There are situations
that require some mechanisms for ensuring confidentiality
and discretion, even in public bodies and in taxpayer funded
agencies.[31] Given the trends that are outlined here, it is likely
that struggles over information freedom and open data will
not only continue but will also ratchet up. This is partly
because dependence on electronically handled information is
a global phenomenon.

The NSA's Global Tentacles

Unsurprisingly, the initial headlines arising from Snowden's NSA revelations centred on the US. The shock value was primarily from knowing that American citizens at home had been swept up in domestic mass surveillance, without ever having been suspected of anything. But it quickly became clear that many other nations and their citizens were implicated and involved. If it was not evident before, the facts were now striking: NSA surveillance is global in scope.

No one was exempt, it seems. First, each of the Five Eyes of the agreement between the US, Australia, Canada, New Zealand and the UK is subject to mass surveillance, initiated by the NSA. Beyond this, allies such as Brazil, Denmark, Germany, France, India, Israel, Italy, Netherlands, Norway, Spain and others were affected and each has its own – sometimes outraged – response. Lastly, countries regarded as unfriendly to the US, such as China, Iran and Russia, are also subject to large-scale surveillance by the NSA.

The spying has direct effects in the countries involved, especially in conflict zones such as those in the Middle East. For example, such surveillance helped to enable the assault on Gaza in 2014. Often working with Canada's CSE and the UK's GCHQ, the NSA has in recent years increased support, sometimes covertly, for the Israeli SIGINT – Signals Intelligence – National Unit, including data used to target and monitor Palestinians. Such activities do not sit well with the US stance of 'brokering peace' in the Middle East. As a NSA document dated 13 April 2013 states, the 'NSA maintains a far-reaching technical and analytic relationship with the Israeli SIGINT National Unit (ISNU) sharing information on access, intercept, targeting, language, analysis and reporting'.[32]

African countries are also in the NSA mix. GCHQ and the NSA targets organizations like the United Nations Development Programme, UNICEF and the charity Médecins du Monde, which all work in conflict zones, especially in Africa. Sixty countries are named in one Snowden document, which also includes details of leaders being targeted, such as Mohamed Ibn Chambas, the African Union/United Nations joint special representative for Darfur, along with many African heads of state.

In one month alone, a Snowden-disclosed system known as 'Boundless Informant' showed that the NSA's Global Access Unit had collected data on over 97 billion emails and 124 billion phone calls, from nearly every country. Three billion items of intelligence were collected on American citizens in February 2013 alone.[33] Boundless Informant is an overview program that tracks ongoing intelligence gathering around the world. The NSA has claimed that it did not really know exactly how extensive its programs were; Boundless Informant offered 'near real-time' statistics on just that.

It must be stressed again that the NSA and its partners touch the lives of millions outside the US. The Five Eyes agreement started as part of a secret treaty between the UK and the US in 1941 and was formalized in 1946. As the Cold War intensified, Australia, Canada and New Zealand were added in the 1950s. So secret was it that, for example, it was not until a raid on the Australian Security Intelligence Organization (ASIO) in 1973 that Gough Whitlam, then Prime Minister, became aware of the UK–US treaty. In New Zealand, on 2 December 1987, then Prime Minister David Lange announced the building of a new intelligence facility, the Waihopai Station. He stressed his country's independence in intelligence work, unaware that a US-dominated system had been present for years, operating the UK–US Echelon system in New Zealand. Although the basis of the agreement concerns common interests and information sharing, the Snowden disclosures made clear that the NSA plays a key role.

Canada, as geographically closest to the US, and for historical reasons having extensive intelligence ties with the US, is often the first to bear the brunt of NSA surveillance. In 2013 – as noted in the Introduction – Snowden documents were released showing how the CSE had collaborated with the NSA, allowing that agency to use the US Embassy in Ottawa as a base for espionage during the 2010 G8 and G20 summit meetings. The Briefing Notes leaked in the secret documents showed that the NSA's plans were 'closely coordinated with the Canadian partner'.[34]

The precise targets were not made clear but in 2009 a similar event with the G20 in London, England, involved hacking the phone calls and emails of foreign politicians and diplomats. In Canada, say the Briefing Notes, the NSA was tasked with 'providing support to policy-makers' and 'US policy goals' – presumably to give the US and Canada an advantage in any negotiations. It appears that the CSE was outsourcing work to the NSA that it would be illegal for CSE to do, namely, to spy on Canadian citizens in Canada. With no evidence of terrorist threats, the NSA warned of 'issue-based extremists' engaged in vandalism. And while this touches the lives of 'citizens' and thus shows disrespect for democratic practices, it again raises the question of invidious distinctions: why should anyone be subject to such generalized surveillance?

Other effects of NSA surveillance in Canada are less obvious, however. For example, few are aware of how far 'internal' internet routing in Canada – city-to-city, for instance – actually goes through the US, where it is susceptible to NSA interception. And because submarine fibre-optic cables travel primarily between the US and Europe, international internet traffic to and from Canada also goes through the US via NSA installations.[35] This reliance on US infrastructure compromises Canadian sovereignty and of course, Canadians' privacy rights. It deviates markedly from a historic Canadian commitment to independent communications. Due to the Prism program, Canadians using major internet companies such as Google or Facebook are now vulnerable to NSA scrutiny as their sometimes sensitive data journey through cloud and network services in the US.

As for the 'internal' routing issue, University of Toronto researchers on the IXmaps project have tracked the routes of data packets which frequently go through NSA internet surveillance sites. Computer scientist Andrew Clement refers to this as 'boomerang traffic'. Even a message from his office to the provincial government buildings, a few blocks away in downtown Toronto, will be routed through Chicago or New York, either of which means data go through a suspected NSA centre. The process depends on cooperation between the NSA and corporate personnel to splice optical 'splitters' that allow the data to flow but simultaneously mirror copies for NSA storage. Not only who communicates, but what they say, whether they are engaged in online banking or communicating with a government department, is thus at risk.[36]

Surveillance and the Future of the Internet

The politics of the internet is central in the era of mass surveillance. In an obvious sense, this has been a key aspect of the Snowden controversies from the outset. Governments around the world, including prominently the US Administration,[37] have been obliged to respond to the continuing debates over state power and its entwinement with commercial networks, especially internet companies. They are building on internet-and-surveillance expertise developed over several decades.

In Europe, for example, an international and independent commission to inquire into the future of the internet after the Snowden revelations was announced in January 2014. Headed by Carl Bildt, the former Swedish Prime Minister and the Foreign Minister at the time, it reports in 2016. The commission has 25 members including former intelligence officials, academics and politicians and its brief relates both to the control of the internet by authoritarian regimes and also to the 'nature and extent of online surveillance' that have 'led to a loss of trust'.[38] In April 2014, Snowden himself addressed a meeting of the Parliamentary Assembly of the Council of Europe, which produced a report published in January 2015. It says the Snowden revelations are 'stunning', states that mass surveillance has a chilling effect on basic freedoms and deplores the 'deliberate weakening of internet security' by surveillance agencies that use back doors and exploit weak security standards.[39]

The politics of internet surveillance is also a strong current running through the internet companies themselves – they have had to distance themselves from the NSA while at the same time acknowledging that they do, usually under legal constraint, cooperate extensively with government. Alongside these areas of turbulence is the active resistance of numerous non-governmental organizations which are engaged with both the civil liberties and privacy dimensions of mass surveillance and, again, the future of the internet itself.

The new coalitions that have formed since Snowden between well-established groups such as the Electronic Privacy Information Center, the Electronic Frontier Foundation and the American Civil Liberties Union in the US, for instance, or Privacy International, based in the UK, or

OpenMedia in Canada, are making waves in fresh ways and building creatively towards consensus on each new Snowden revelation. Many have hoped for a more united response to surveillance, perhaps one that could become a social movement, similar to environmentalism. It is not clear that such a day has dawned[40] or that if it did, it would have the hoped-for impact. Among other things, pointing out to internet companies the sheer costs of their operations that benefit government surveillance may be an equally effective strategy in the short term.

Many people and governments around the world were shaken by the Snowden revelations. Is the internet free in any sense? Is anything secure online? What is the appropriate way of governing these powerful networks? These questions have been raised with increasing urgency, sometimes in relation to major events such as the so-called Arab Spring of 2011–12. Popular political movements attempted to bring down authoritarian regimes – and in some ways succeeded, especially in North Africa. Many Western countries applauded the possibilities for democratic participation and mobilization afforded by the mobile internet, mediated through cellphones. But the governments in question also had sophisticated tools at their disposal to block communications and to identify those considered troublemakers and ringleaders.

The struggles over the internet are global, deep-seated and often bitter. The US, through its intelligence agencies, seems to be competing with dark authoritarian regimes in its development of mass surveillance and its undermining of privacy and civil liberties. The Five Eyes partners collude with the US, ensuring that the surveillance net is cast very widely around the world. India and China have their own powerful surveillance systems, and argue for their own versions of 'cyber-sovereignty' (neither of which leaves much scope for limiting undemocratic government control of the internet). Hope for internet freedom and for simple privacy and human rights seems to be dimmed by what we now know about global mass surveillance.

In the US issues of internet and communications surveillance often focus on the Foreign Intelligence Surveillance Act because much of what Snowden has revealed hangs on a reinterpretation of that law. Little altered in FISA between 1978 and 2001, but after 9/11 several changes were made by the secretive Foreign Intelligence Surveillance Court, especially the addition of Section 215. This expanded the scope of FISA orders compelling third parties to hand over to government things like business records.[41]

There was also a 'Raw Take' order in 2002 that weakened restrictions on sharing information about Americans with foreign governments.[42] And apparently minor changes in wording, applied in 2007 and incorporated in the FISA Amendment Act in 2008, made a big difference to what data could be collected. In some 'Foreign Content' and 'Domestic Content' documents revealed by Snowden, the word 'facilities', previously referring to phone numbers or email addresses, was stretched to include gateways to global communication networks in and out of the US. The post-9/11 expansion of permissible activities, by whatever means, subtly changed the face of global surveillance.

When Snowden's revelations burst into world news, many assumed that the NSA's activities were simply illegal. The moral outrage expressed by Snowden spread quickly when the issues seemed crystal clear. However, as the details came to light of how FISA was surreptitiously reinterpreted and as lawyers have come to contrary rulings about the legality of what goes on at the NSA, strident opposition to global mass surveillance has been muffled by a mass of technical and legal ambiguities. Without doubt, laws have been reinterpreted behind closed doors – a moral issue in itself – but the upshot of the legal wrangling is that attention is deflected from the enormity of their effects – making millions of people subject to mass surveillance.

The picture is not one of unrelieved gloom, however. Brazilian President Dilma Rousseff, whose phone was tapped by the NSA, addressed the UN General Assembly in September 2013, arguing for some straightforward rules for the internet. Someone with a past like hers – an activist against the totalitarian military dictatorship in Brazil – is sensitive to surveillance issues. She declared that privacy is vital to freedom of expression and opinion and thus to democracy itself. And, pointedly, she observed that the right to safety and security of citizens of one country may never be guaranteed by violating the basic human rights of citizens of another country.

Germany joined Brazil in sponsoring a UN resolution on the right to privacy – the first for 25 years.[43] At home, Brazil enacted a Digital Bill of Rights (Marco Civil da Internet) based on the idea of net neutrality which, though flawed in the eyes of some critics, is at least a step in the right direction. Brazil also insists on a 'multi-stakeholder' approach to internet governance and hosted a 'NetMundial' meeting to show how this inclusive decision-making model could work. In November 2014 the United Nations released a statement reaffirming the right to privacy in a digital age.[44]

The future of the internet still hangs in the balance as the revelations about mass surveillance continue. As Ron Deibert indicates in *Black Code*, far more than privacy or even just communications are involved here.[45] Broad issues of enclosure – that is, information withheld from the public in media corporations or in centralized government hands – secrecy and the arms race are all implicated. As he says, the Snowden Files 'have blown wide open intricate details of programs that operate deep in the shadows of the classified world, hidden from not only most citizens but from lawmakers too'.

'We are at a crossroads' is a phrase Deibert repeats several times. Analysis of the spread of surveillance has never been more significant, from the threats to individual people to the consequences for war and peace, wealth and poverty, on a global level. Whether from countries such as Brazil, or from the Council of Europe, which has for years attempted to address surveillance – especially since Snowden – some new framework for surveillance is badly needed that speaks to the global character of digital communications and the current lack of adequate rules and oversight for the tracking of domestic and foreign citizens – and that might even query such distinctions.[46]

Having looked at the big picture of the revelations and their global impact, however, it is now time to investigate the impact on ordinary people in their everyday lives. The big picture is indispensable for grasping how large-scale, intensive and invidious are the practices that have been revealed by Snowden and how they touch governments and businesses across the globe, raising the stakes for those attempting to find ways of governing this Janus-faced creature, the internet.

But for most of us, tracing our little paths through daily life at home, work, school and play, or maybe taking trips using transit, trains or planes, such matters may seem distant, out of reach. Here is the problem: it is precisely those little paths through daily life, in each situation in which we find ourselves, that are the stuff of surveillance. Where we are, when, and in touch with whom are the fragments of information known as 'metadata'. So in the next chapter we turn to metadata, which, though it sounds equally huge, is in reality about the micro-details of all our lives.

3

MENACING METADATA

Metadata is extraordinarily intrusive. As an analyst, I would prefer to be looking at metadata than looking at content, because it's quicker and easier, and it doesn't lie.

Edward Snowden, September 2014

In 2009 Malte Spitz, a German Green Party politician, sued Deutsche Telekom to hand over six months of telephone metadata, which he then sent to *Zeit Online*. They in turn combined the geolocation data with his political life, such as Twitter feeds, blog entries and websites, all freely available on the internet. The result is a detailed diary of where he was when, with whom and who else was present. It is an animated reconstruction of his daily life. While the content of his calls may have revealed some important elements of his life, the context yielded by the metadata is far richer. It shows 'our importance to each other, our interests, values and the various roles we play'.[1]

Few had heard the word 'metadata' before the Snowden revelations began. But it soon became a public battleground for debate over the mass surveillance activities of the NSA. The term metadata sounds drily boring but its apparent innocence is deceiving. Many inferences may be made from traffic data, numbers called and duration times. But this does not necessarily make metadata the perfect anti-terror tool. Its security use has yet to demonstrate clear positive results. And the downsides of the use of metadata are many. It puts innocent lives at risk and damages democratic norms governing potentially intrusive state activities. For some, metadata is menacing.

The White House claimed during 2013 that more than 50 terror plots had been uncovered by the NSA's trawling methods. But this was queried by a White House NSA review panel[2] in December that year and by an independent analysis by the New America Foundation in January 2014. This latter report showed that of 225 cases of terrorist activity that the NSA said were investigated, only four were the result of using phone metadata and knowing of those four did not prevent any attacks. The report concluded that 'Surveillance of American phone metadata has had no discernible impact on preventing acts of terrorism and only the most marginal of impacts on preventing terrorist-related activity, such as fundraising for a terrorist group.'[3]

This does not mean that metadata has had no 'successes', however. In one case, a former FBI agent was brought to trial for releasing classified information about a CIA operation in Yemen to a journalist with Associated Press. Phone metadata was the key to finding him. Only three leaks prosecutions had ever occurred under previous US presidents. Eight have already happened during the Obama years.[4] As with so many surveillance systems, metadata may fail in meeting its

ostensible objectives but it has many other uses beyond what
it is promoted for.

Metadata is increasingly used in contexts where 'big data'
practices have been adopted. Snowden candidly comments in
a June 2013 interview on video that the NSA 'targets the
communications of everyone...and filters, analyses, measures them and stores them for periods of time'.[5] Backed up
by the documents he disclosed, this demonstrates how big
data spells surveillance today. 'Collect it all' is the gung-ho
slogan of the NSA and other intelligence agencies, waiting
with their software experts and statisticians to run tests on as
much data as they can. 'Data analytics' is the technical term
for discovering meaningful patterns in the data deluge. Or to
change from that liquid metaphor, data analysis holds hope
for finding the proverbial needle in the haystack. Bigger
haystacks, paradoxically, bring needles more readily to light.
Or so they say.

Big data, frequently hyped as the next big thing to transform the way we think about the world, is at the heart of the
surveillance state revealed by Snowden. The future of the
internet is clearly up for grabs in the sense that its democratic
potential and promise of open communication fall under
what is perceived as the dark shadow of surveillance. The way
data are handled is a related but different problem. The key
idea here is that new things can be learned from a very large
body of data that cannot be learned with less. This notion
does have traction in some areas but, perhaps ill-advisedly, it
has been adopted wholesale in many intelligence agencies.
No wonder the 'collect it all' mantra echoes around the
world's communication security centres.

This chapter examines the relationship between Snowden's disclosures on the one hand, and metadata, big data
surveillance and its capacities and consequences, on the other.
Surveillance today cannot be understood without a sense of

how the quest for 'big data' approaches are becoming increasingly central. This is dramatically demonstrated by the Snowden revelations.

Big Data, Big Brother?

So what is big data? It is not so much a very large entity as a way of doing things. It refers to ways of handling data, to practices and processes. You start with large datasets and then search through them, cluster them according to what you are looking for, and cross-reference them to find fresh patterns.[6] To do so, you draw on metaphors to capture the idea of what you are doing, along with software and statistical techniques to actually crunch the numbers. All sorts of agencies use big data techniques and part of the problem lies right there. What may seem relatively harmless in one area – say Amazon. com's use of big data techniques to suggest books or music you may like – may be quite inappropriate, even risky, in another.

That is, some uses of big data may actually make some people more vulnerable, and 'big data surveillance' is just one such area. In practice, big data has a close association with Big Brother – or rather his twenty-first century digital descendants. The question before us is how far big data intensifies certain surveillance trends associated with information technologies and networks[7] and is thus concerned with emerging configurations of power and influence that are revealed, especially post-Snowden.

Like any other process, surveillance changes constantly and the application of big data techniques is one such driver of change at present. Classical studies of surveillance, following the work of French historian Michel Foucault, focused on surveillance as a way of creating discipline. People may alter their behaviour when they know they are being watched, especially in enclosed locations such as prisons or factories. But the use of networked technologies that pick up traces from devices and aggregate fragmented data permits the surveillance of more mobile populations, well beyond specific spaces. In this case, the emphasis is more on controlling behaviour – for example, through access to buildings, online sites, privileges – than discipline.[8]

Such a shift is also associated with the steady move of surveillance from targeted scrutiny of groups and individuals to mass monitoring in search of patterns of relationship that is sometimes called 'actionable intelligence'.[9] Big data surveillance exemplifies this, particularly in the ways revealed by Snowden. The connections have been evident for some time,[10] but Snowden's revelations have brought them into the public eye as never before. Both new trends, and the expansion of older ones, come into view.

Snowden's Oxymoron: 'Targeting Everyone'

If things at the NSA are bad, suggests Snowden, things elsewhere could be worse. In the UK, the Tempora program 'snarfed everything', said Snowden in a *Der Spiegel* interview.[11] Tempora appears to be even more like a dragnet as it acts as a 'full-take' internet buffer, meaning that not merely metadata but complete messages and other data records were sucked into GCHQ to be retained for three full days and, if necessary, shared with the NSA. There are also Upstream's joint cable and network tapping abilities, which can intercept any internet traffic. Then there is XKeyscore, with its database that allows the information to be extracted in real time.[12] The dark humour here is that 'targeting' is what national security surveillance used to be about. By definition, it was relatively limited in scope. To 'target everyone' is an oxymoron.

The surveillance practices revealed by Snowden show clearly – if not completely – that governments – American, British, Canadian and others – engage in astonishingly large-scale monitoring of populations, and, even more significantly, how they do it. On the one hand, the NSA engages contractors to share the burden of their work and also gathers and mines user data collected by other corporations, especially telephone, internet and web companies. And on the other hand, this kind of surveillance also means that the NSA and similar agencies watch for cookies and log-in information connected with our routine, daily use of the internet.

They thus use data derived from the use of devices such as cellphones or geo-locating social media sites. What users unknowingly disclose on those platforms – such as Facebook or Twitter – or when using their phones, is usable data for 'national security' and policing purposes. But more importantly, metadata relating to users is gleaned without their knowledge from when they simply switch on their machines.

Remember, much may be learned from metadata. Yves-Alexandre de Montjoye, at the Massachusetts Institute of Technology, checked three months of credit card records, scrubbed of numbers and names, from 1.1 million users in an unnamed country. For 90 per cent of people, the researchers were able to identify the card holders from just four bits of information – a tweet, an Instagram pic and the like. This was a follow-up from a similar study of mobile phone records, in 2013, in which 95 per cent of people could be identified from their phone records.[13]

Once again, note the three significant actors in this drama: government agencies, private corporations, and, though unwittingly, ordinary users. What holds these groups together, in a sense, is the software, the algorithms, the codes that allow users' data to be systematically extracted or disclosed, analysed and turned into what the data gatherers and others, such as the NSA, hope will be actionable data. Unfortunately few non-technically trained people understand the ways that algorithms actually work and what their social and ethical impacts are.[14]

What is clear is that algorithms are central to the (big) data practices that different kinds of intelligence operations have in common. And while algorithms may formally be a set of procedures for finding solutions to a given problem, they never act on their own, even if they are often thought of as 'black boxes'. They are part of a complex – an assemblage would be a suitable technical term – that works *with* their users to produce outcomes. They can also be repurposed and redeployed for tasks beyond their original intention. In other words, algorithms are controlled even though they can be mobilized to, as it were, act alone.

As Snowden himself said in the June 2013 video quoted above, the NSA targets the communications of everyone and then filters, analyses, measures them and stores them for periods of time because it is the easiest, most efficient and most valuable way of achieving these ends. Clearly, algorithmic analysis is vital to this process. But because we do not fully understand the workings of algorithms, however, a phrase like Snowden's raises more questions than it answers.

What can be said is that the NSA depends on codes, the algorithms, plus the witting or unwitting cooperation of both telephone and internet corporations in order to do surveillance. Individual users may play a part, too, as they work and play on social media platforms and use their smartphones. But their role is hardly one of fully conscious actors in the drama, even though their awareness may increase over time. This already goes beyond what many once imagined was still the conventional, direct and specifically targeted surveillance by state agencies of individuals, to mass surveillance, dependent on a close liaison with corporate bodies and on the self-recording devices used in everyday communications and transactions. The gathering of national intelligence in the US is a mammoth undertaking, worth around US$70 billion per year[15] and involving extensive links with universities, internet companies, social media and outside contractors – such as Booz Allen Hamilton that employed Edward Snowden when Snowden illegally conducted his removal of sensitive data. If nothing else, the economic value of these operations indicates how much emphasis is placed on data processing by government agencies and in turn by global corporations. But what kinds of data are sucked up so avidly by these organizations with such sophisticated processing power?

Metadata Meddling

Metadata takes many forms, well beyond communications. For example, automatic vehicle licence plate recognition systems or word-processing programs also generate metadata.[16] While specific cases of monitoring the content of phone calls and examining text messages exist as well, the extremely large-scale collection and analysis of metadata characterizes many of the disclosures about the kinds of activities with which the NSA is engaged. When the Snowden revelations began in June 2013, governments and intelligence agencies were quick to dismiss them by downplaying the significance of metadata.

In the US, the collection of metadata was permitted after 9/11 under the FISC 'Section 215 Bulk telephony metadata program', but it is unclear how far similar programs extend to other countries such as Canada or the UK. However, John

Forster, the head of Canada's CSE, declared before a Senate hearing in February 2014 that metadata – 'essential to CSEC's work' – is collected and stored in Canada, although he did not comment on how it is used or shared.[17] It was also revealed in 2014 that the Canada Border Services Agency (CBSA) made 19,000 requests for subscriber data in one year. But this and other related Canadian agencies are under no statutory requirement to say how often such requests are made or for how much data.[18]

In 2014, a story appeared in the news media that Canada's CSE had collected data from airport wifi systems. In fact, it was a general means of identifying travel patterns and geographic locations using ID data – that is, metadata – in conjunction with a database of IP addresses supplied by the company Quova over a two-week period in January 2014. Such metadata may be used, for instance, to set up an alarm when a 'suspect' enters a particular hotel, or to check on someone – a kidnapper, maybe – who may have repeatedly visited a particular location. But it takes little imagination to think of other potential uses for such datasets.

This is why security critic Bruce Schneier cuts through the obscurity to state unequivocally that 'metadata is surveillance'. As he also observes, while mass media accounts focus on *what* surveillance data are being collected, the most significant question is *how* the NSA analyses those data.[19] This again means trying to understand the software, the algorithms, that manage the analysis. What is known is this. On the one hand, the nearly 5 billion cellphone records collected by the NSA each day by tapping into cables that connect mobile networks globally can reveal personal data about where users are located, anywhere in the world. As we saw in the case of Malte Spitz, daily life events, contacts and patterns can be readily reconstructed from metadata. The NSA can attempt to track individuals to private homes and can also retrace earlier journeys, whenever the phone is on, because phones transmit location data whether or not they are in use. On the other hand, the NSA also analyses *patterns* of behaviour to reveal more personal information and relationships between different users.[20] The latter is more subtle, but in the big data world, more significant.

These pattern-seeking processes are the ones where big data practices really come into their own. For example, the NSA program known as Co-Traveler uses highly sophisticated mathematical techniques to map cellphone users' relationships, superimposing them on others to find significant intersections and correlations. Co-Traveler is meant to search for the associates of foreign intelligence targets, although domestic users' data are also garnered 'incidentally' and the foreign sweeps are so broad that they are bound to include Americans on a mass scale. This is the searching, aggregating and cross-referencing process referred to above that characterizes some of the technical aspects of big data.

So, yes, metadata may be menacing; the apparently trivial may in some cases be terrifying. But for many of us, most of the time, metadata may well be inconsequential, even beneficial. In the hands of the NSA and its partners, however, it can also be a means of misidentification and worse. In Canada, as in the US, UK and other countries, fragments of data have been mistakenly interpreted in ways that, after 9/11, led to egregious renditions of innocent citizens to foreign countries for torture and needless interrogation.

The kinds of algorithms used, the piecing together of fragments of unconnected data, often based on stereotypical assumptions about people from particular backgrounds, may create apparently incriminating profiles that are readily seized upon by those taught to think that citizens-in-general may be masquerading as terrorists. People with no criminal

record, who have done no wrong and have nothing to hide
may yet have much to fear.

Big Data Surveillance

The big data/surveillance link was recognized by US President Obama on 17 January 2014 when he called for a 'com-
prehensive review of big data and privacy' following the
Snowden leaks.[21] It was acknowledged when the US proposed new rules governing bulk data collection by the NSA
of the phone-calling habits of Americans.[22] The once-secret
bulk phone records problem was what had most alarmed
privacy advocates when the Snowden leaks began in 2013 and
now the President proposed that it should be curtailed, along
the lines of a European data retention directive. It is not
clear, however, that the big data aspects of the bulk phone
records were entirely understood.

Surveillance constantly undergoes change and is currently
morphing in several new ways, some of which alter its character. Different kinds of data are now being captured and
used in new ways, which prompts some to distinguish between
surveillance as targeted practices over against new forms of
what is often called 'dataveillance'.[23] The concept of 'dataveillance' was coined by Roger Clarke, almost 30 years ago,
to describe the surveillance of someone's activities by studying their data trail. Today, this includes not only things like
credit card purchases or social insurance claims but also cellphone calls, biometrics capture and internet use.[24]

Not only are data captured differently, they are also processed, combined and analysed in new ways. Social media,
which appeared on the scene at roughly the same time as
responses to 9/11, are now the source of much data, used not
only for commercial but also for 'security' purposes. They

therefore boosted the 'surveillance state'. One current buzz-word is 'datafication', which points to the ways in which, for many businesses, the information infrastructure is their heart[25] Ordinary users' social activities are gathered as data, quantified and classified, making possible real-time tracking and monitoring. Needless to say, few pause to consider how their data trails multiply as they are constantly in touch, and online.

It goes beyond this, however. With big data practices, for example, personal data – now including identifiable metadata – are not collected for certain limited, specified and transparent purposes, a restriction which is the goal of data protection and privacy advocates. Rather, big data reverses the order of prior policing or intelligence activities that would conventionally have targeted suspects or persons of interest and *then* sought data about them, with courts authorizing interceptions or searches. Now bulk data are obtained and data are aggregated from different sources *before* determining the full range of their actual and potential uses, and algorithms and analytics are mobilized not only to understand a past sequence of events but also to predict and intervene *before* behaviours, events and processes have been set in motion. For instance, all major financial transactions and all airline passenger data are analysed. This is the *Minority Report*, 'pre-crime' effect again. Both its corporate and government aspects raise questions for analysis and critique.

Such pre-emptive approaches in security and policing, depending on prediction, are nothing new. They have been growing steadily since the 1990s. The search for terrorist suspects after 9/11 offered further temptation to over-collect data. Perhaps even more important to cost-cutting government departments, the falling cost of processing power is a strong inducement to use new data analytics in a number of fields.[26] Promises abound that real-time data analytics will

transform aspects of retail, manufacturing, healthcare and
public sector organizations. Security and policing are just one
of many areas affected by this two-sided trend. Celebrating
the supposed successes of big data dominates the airspace and
critical questions are all too often treated as noise to be
eliminated.

The differences between big data applications are crucial
here. For example, Ian Kerr and Jessica Earle distinguish
helpfully between three kinds of prediction: consequential,
where one aim is to help clients or users to choose what is
likely to be beneficial to them; preferential, illustrated by
marketers trying to second-guess our desires from our browsing behaviour; and pre-emptive, where there is a deliberate
intention to reduce someone's range of options.[27] In the
context of law and justice, the last raises fundamental issues
of privacy and due process. Where legal systems are based
on an after-the-fact system of penalties or punishments, the
turn to one based on future-oriented preventative measures
is a game changer, not least for those rendered unable to
understand or contribute meaningfully to the process.

Big Data Capacities

The term 'big data' suggests that size is its key feature.
Massive quantities of data about people and their activities
are indeed generated by big data practices and many corporate and government bodies – not least the NSA, GCHQ and
the rest – wish to capitalize on what is understood as the big
data boom. However, the prominent idea of large size both
yields important clues and, on its own, can mislead. While
the *capacities* of big data practices (including the use of metadata) intensify surveillance by expanding interconnected
datasets and analytical tools, this tells only a part of the story.

First, where does that 'big' data come from? Information researcher Rob Kitchin distinguishes between three kinds, each of which may be applied in surveillance contexts: directed, automated and volunteered.[28] In the first, a human operator obtains the data, obvious examples being CCTV systems or an intelligence agency seeking, say, vehicle ownership records. In the second, the data are gathered without a human operator intervening; traces are recorded routinely from transactions with banks or consumer outlets and communications, using cellphones above all. As we have seen, there are several examples of this in NSA work. In the third, data are in a weak sense 'volunteered' by the user, who gives out information on social media sites and the like. Of course, social media users do not necessarily think of their activities in terms of volunteering data to third parties,[29] but this is an accurate way of understanding surveillance data gathering in this context.

Understood this way, the capacities of big data surveillance take on some new meanings. The enthusiasm for commercial uses of big data is shared by those in the security field, thus stimulating further integration of these activities. In a big data intelligence context, the same data, gathered by internet companies for marketing, is increasingly used for different purposes, such as tracking terror suspects or environmental protesters. The change of context might well alter how social media users (the 'data subjects' in regulation-speak) might construe their privacy or how legal limits on secondary use might be stretched. But beyond this, the same commercial data may be given *new meanings* in the security realm, combined and connected in novel ways.

What the Snowden revelations show is that big data practices allow operators to infer individual or group characteristics relating to security from a context of consumer marketing. Data researcher Louise Amoore calls this kind of reasoning 'data derivatives'.[30] In the security-surveillance context such associations and links, however trivial and improbable, may be given new meanings that are cut off from the values that once made sense of them, and of course from the people whose activities generated them in the first place.

Big Data Consequences

It is clear from the Snowden disclosures that there are several ways in which commitment to big data practices seems to be shifting the emphasis of surveillance. There seem to be three imperatives at work: automate, anticipate and adapt.

Automate

Much surveillance, including the best-known kind, using video cameras, is now automated. That is, the system works without real-time reliance on human operators. The combination of readily available software and its relatively low price is an incentive to choose technical solutions over more labour-intensive ones in surveillance practices as in other fields. This means that automated surveillance will become increasingly possible. At the same time, greater data storage capacity means that larger and larger amounts of data are collected before their use has been ascertained,[31] with consequences which are as yet unknown. What we do know, however, is that whoever makes decisions about algorithms and datasets will have the capacity to make a difference in these emerging scenarios.[32]

The automation of surveillance is also an aspect of the way that surveillance occurs as a routine management procedure rather than as a sinister state conspiracy to keep close watch on all citizens. While big data practices may be seen clearly in the case of the NSA, they are also commonplace elsewhere. The automating of surveillance is part of the kinds of cost-cutting and efficiency exercises that have dominated public administration for decades. Aware of the expense of large-scale surveillance, many organizations from the 1990s onwards found the growing availability of automated processes very attractive. Lots of rather partial and disconnected projects now try to harness new technologies in the name of knowing service-users better and more efficient government.[33] The consequences appear conspiratorial and may have undesirable aspects, but in many cases this was probably not planned.

What databases do is to create profiles of individuals and groups based on their activities, connections, performances, transactions and movements that relate to, among other things, government departments. These data 'make up' the people seen in the system, in ways that are constantly shifting, fluctuating. In this way, a market-based or neoliberal logic of control fits neatly with the ways that individuals are 'made up' by data. If the role of 'data doubles' in determining the life-chances and choices of individuals is a major concern[34] then its big data magnification will likely intensify such concerns. The affected populations will experience more 'errors' that produce risky outcomes for individuals and groups. As we understand it better, it will also be contested more effectively.

The kind of 'soft' surveillance power associated with big data is at work in marketing, in ways that are parallel to and sometimes interrelated with those 'harder' forms found in 'national security'. Both enterprises work with collected data to try to identify likely targets, whether that is to tempt them to purchase a product or to single them out as possible wrongdoers. Marketing went beyond its conventional demographic measures – 'we know where you live' was their slogan[35] – to more psychographic categories, measuring mental states, in the later 1990s, and then, as marketing went online, it was able to use search histories to create further consumer clustering, superimposed on the former categories. Algorithms are used increasingly to target particular kinds of consumers in relation more to real-time web use than to the older categories of census and postcode (or zipcode). This contributes to cybernetic-type control, where what is assumed to be normal and correct behaviour is embedded in circuits of consumer (or employment, health or education) practices. This is also highly significant for what Snowden has revealed.

The emphasis on databases calls for a shift in focus from some accounts that refer more directly to organizations and individuals, to ones that acknowledge – as privacy advocates and others have argued for some time – that online subjects are also difficult to define. Ordinary users of social media and the internet are not just the individual 'atoms' that some older privacy theories suggest. They are, like most people, already enmeshed in a variety of relationships – daughter, teacher, friend, neighbour, insurer – that help to define them. Some are very engaged, politically, and frequently work together to raise questions about big data surveillance in the political realm. Human rights codes and constitutional documents do recognize privacy, of course, but keeping these in view is a constant challenge.

Some crucial shifts are occurring in the ways that surveillance is carried out and experienced. Much surveillance today is mobile and invisible and depends on the involuntary participation of individuals who may not guess that they are carrying what I call a 'PTD' – Personal Tracking Device – which is effectively what cellphones are. But because cellphones are 'hybrid' technologies they foster contradictory concepts of 'personal data'. From a billing perspective, companies use cellphone data precisely because they refer to identifiable persons. But from a regulatory viewpoint, the data are 'anonymous'.[36] Equally, if we use a tablet or laptop, how could we know that log-in details or our IP address would be crucial aspects of metadata that can be used to track us? Equally, how could we guess that those fragments of metadata would be used to try to *anticipate* our behaviour in ways that are now overwhelmingly evident in the Snowden disclosures?[37] Surveillance today is *both* top-down, in classic state surveillance style, *and* also sideways or, even 'diagonal'[38] in its attempt to control access to both physical and online spaces.

Surveillance in the era of big data, then, does not focus only on the body or on a population but on definitions to which we may contribute as part of our daily online interactions. It 'makes up' the data double, our online persona, and that entity then acts back on those with whom the data are associated, informing us who we are, what we should desire or hope for, including whom we should become. The algorithms grip us even as they follow us, producing ever more information to try to make the user data more effective. Users discover, one might say, that the price of our freedom in both political and consumer contexts is our shaping or conditioning by algorithms.

Big data practices in general encourage the use of automated decision-making and thus downplay the role of human discretion. Seen in classic liberal-legal terms, automated decisions made in government systems can easily deprive individuals of their liberty and property, triggering calls for 'due process' or 'fair treatment' in the judicial system. For example, in the US, computers can terminate individuals' Medicaid benefits, taking away a statutorily granted property interest. Innocent individuals may be designated as dead-beat parents, resulting in lost property, revoked driving and professional licences, and injury to their reputations.[39]

The US federal government's 'No Fly' data-matching program labels some individuals as potential terrorists, resulting in the postponement or denial of air travel, both significant impairments of liberty rights. Automation, suggests Danielle Citron, will be a driving force in the retreat from the discretionary model of administrative law.[40] Nonetheless, due process does mean that citizens or consumers can push back against such automation when it prevents or limits understanding or responding to suspicions, charges or cut benefits. However, such an assumption depends on those citizens and consumers knowing what is happening, which big data approaches make very difficult if not impossible.

Anticipate

The political-economic and socio-technical responses to 9/11 helped to change the 'tense' of surveillance in some significant ways.[41] Once, surveillance relied extensively on past records to build a picture of the suspicious person or the susceptible purchaser. Steadily, as real-time records of the present have proliferated, it has become increasingly possible to know what is going on *at the time*. And while, since at least the 1990s, risk management techniques had increasingly turned towards attempts to predict and pre-empt future developments, the anticipatory approach was ratcheted up some further notches as early forms of data analytics were brought into play.

The frequently advertised notion of 'connecting the dots' is based on what more technically is 'anticipatory analytics'. Here, the aim of amassing and mining data is 'knowledge discovery', finding patterns in data that would point a suspicious finger towards persons and groups whose associations or communications add up to a likely 'person of interest' profile, as in the well-known TV show. The idea is to second-guess what might happen in the future. In other words, not merely what the profile suggests the person might be, but what they might *become*. As Ursula Franklin warned in 1990, 'the technological possibilities for information gathering, storage, and evaluation, interwoven with a tight net of administrative infrastructures, have made it possible to treat certain parts of the future as parts of the present.'[42] This is now a significant factor in assigning riskiness, from which it is a short step to suspicion.[43]

Big data builds on these already existing modes of surveillance that *anticipate* our actions. Such systems attempt to create new knowledge using the statistical power of large numbers to help grasp the fragmented details of individual lives. The anticipatory approach is common across the range of big data applications. Google Now, for example, uses just this method to draw on a vast ocean of data – organized by their filters – in order to alert specific users to things that may have great importance to them, from warning them about delayed flights to offering early diagnoses of flu.[44] Everyone collects and transmits much usable data, especially using smartphones, but also through using any digital device.

The big mistake, however, is to assume that big data – as in the case of user searches for information about flu – can *substitute* for rather than *supplement* conventional modes of analysis. As it happens, experts demonstrate that the conventional forms of analysis still seem to have a high degree of validity compared with crowd-sourced methods.[45] If this is true of epidemiology how much more care should be taken with risk analysis relating to (another rather elastic concept) 'terrorism'. In this case, unlike that of flu, there is no regular presentation of accurate, identifiable and actionable intelligence. The term 'terrorism' itself is politicized, it is nearly impossible to distinguish between a violent and non-violent activist, and with so few facts, correcting for false positives and negatives is both rickety and risky.

The situation is worsened by the fact that anticipatory approaches are more concerned with 'premediating and pin-pointing potential dangers'[46] and less concerned with the overall picture of a given individual. The problem is that profiles may be built and inferences made about individuals with privacy regulations and data protection in place. The conventional links between data and the individual have become tenuous and torn. How can privacy rights be associated with the fractured and reduced image of a data double?[47] Much filtering and analysis is done, as noted above, *before* identifiable individuals come into sight. The harms in question are not necessarily to individuals as to potential futures, to the very possibility of making a political claim.[48]

Adapt

We saw earlier that many big data practices are common across different platforms. However, what might under some circumstances be acceptable for Google may be highly unacceptable where the NSA is concerned. Google maps and indexes the public web. Its data centres process satellite images and ground-level photos of the built environment in a 'geospatial' database that can be connected to specific individuals and organizations. The electronic activities of hundreds of millions of people, including emails and search requests, are also known by and accessible to Google.

What the NSA does is essentially similar to what Google does – capturing phone-call metadata and gaining access to information – though the NSA works through systems like Tempora and possibly Prism.[49] But the additional factor is that the NSA, using the Foreign Intelligence Surveillance Act, can follow up on 'exceptions' with warrants to check on persons of interest. This has been possible for some time, a fact first exposed by former AT&T employee Mark Klein in 2005, when he showed how AT&T helped the NSA to gain access to its own systems through a splitter that fed into an Intelligence Traffic Analyzer. It was also shown in 2006 that the NSA used its phone-call database for social network analysis. According to information from Snowden in 2013, collection of phone-call data on US citizens to foreign phone numbers is still occurring.

Curiously, solving the problems of data storage and analysis has been key to the operations of Google and Yahoo! This prompted the NSA to improve on Google's BigTable systems with a program called Accumulo, which has multiple levels of security access. That is, different users can be treated differently at what is called 'cell level', with some having more access than others to the same data, while maintaining data confidentiality throughout. It can also generate near real-time reports from data patterns, such as words or addresses from a range of IP addresses, right across the internet. Through what are called 'iterators', patterns emerge that are constantly reported back to the NSA so that it can 'visualize' links between entities based on relationships and attributes.

In this way it resembles Facebook's 'social graph', a global mapping system of users and how they are related to each other. It is the largest social network dataset in the world. Prism offers the NSA access to cloud providers online, primarily seeking metadata, which completes the circle. The NSA's new data centre in Utah,[50] which looks like a large manufacturing facility with its huge data-storage capabilities designed for cybersecurity, will enable the expansion of Prism-type real-time internet surveillance, although, being classified, the precise purposes are unpublished.

One question for privacy advocates and others is whether or not these surveillance operations are legal. Such critics sometimes contend that they violate laws designed to protect the liberty and privacy of citizens. The assurances given, in the US and other countries, that *citizens* are not targeted by these systems have failed to reassure citizens and privacy advocates.[51] It is also clear that some data are 'incidentally' collected on the whereabouts of domestic cellphones. Such data may be used to map users' relationships, as noted earlier in relation to Co-Traveler.

Let me flag the word 'incidental': it raises a key question for privacy and its politics. Metadata, as we have seen, comes from many sources, mainly from the consumer and media-user world. Fragments of data originally collected for purposes such as billing or advertising are repurposed in the hands of the NSA and other security intelligence agencies. Data are used for objectives unrelated to the original reason for gathering them. Basic privacy rules about the specifying the purpose of data collection and letting the person concerned know what is being collected are out the window. We can no longer know what information about us is being tapped by security agencies, let alone consent to its use. What might matter little in the original context could well be consequential in the new one.

It is also crucial to distinguish between different kinds of consequences. Marketing uses of big data analytics cannot simply be extended without qualm to preventing terrorism. Marketers will be satisfied with results that are accurate only in a relatively small proportion of cases, just because the cluster around that group will also be profitable, albeit to a lesser extent. The economic harms to individuals from such inaccuracy, though potentially serious, are seldom considered by marketers.[52] In some contexts, such as when Amazon suggests books in which readers have no interest, the outcomes are fairly inconsequential.

But the attempt to find terrorist 'needles' in big data 'haystacks' is fraught with palpable problems. Such terrorist 'needles' are, generally speaking, clever, determined and imaginative in their attempts to evade detection. The needle-and-haystack argument carries with it a high probability of false positives, meaning individuals can be incorrectly identified as terrorists, which can easily have very harmful impacts on those falsely identified.

Where Next?

Much debate raised by the Snowden revelations has to do with metadata, and by extension, 'big data surveillance'. Snowden revealed much that was previously secret but it must be admitted that what we now know is still unclear. This is because much of what actually happens is in the coded language of software and of algorithms. What we do know fairly clearly, though, is that how data are generated and framed always has decisive effects on the final outcomes of analysis. As Lisa Gitelman, a historian of media, reminds us, 'raw data is an oxymoron'.[53] Data has always been 'cooked'.[54] What we do not fully understand yet is how the recipes – algorithms of data analysis – are made up.

Even terms such as metadata, so crucial to big data surveillance, lack clear definition, even though metadata can generally be distinguished from data such as the content of phone calls or emails. Yet that ill-defined metadata is constantly used by security and intelligence agencies, and the patterns revealed by the algorithms used to filter it relate back to the purposes that shaped the data in the first place and forward to those affected by the designation of groups that may contain persons of interest. Such people will have as little idea as others of what metadata or algorithms are, but they will discover all too sharply in practice what it means to be singled out as a person-of-interest.

All this raises further questions: What are the prospects for privacy in the twenty-first century? Does the concept of privacy encompass all that is challenged – or even threatened – by what we now know about state surveillance, following Snowden? And, when persons of interest concern themselves about privacy, how does this relate to their concerns about civil liberties and human rights – or even about democracy itself? It is these questions that we have to address if we are to complete our analysis of surveillance after Snowden.

4

PRECARIOUS PRIVACY

Your rights matter because you never know when you're going to need them.

Edward Snowden, March 2014

Let me tell you about Faisal Gill. He is a patriotic American, a Republican, served in the Navy, had high-level security clearance when he worked for the Department of Homeland Security under George W. Bush, works in his community, sent his children to a Catholic school, is a lawyer. It was revealed by Edward Snowden through Glenn Greenwald on 9 July 2014 that the NSA and the FBI have been covertly monitoring his emails under secretive procedures intended to target terrorists and foreign spies.[1]

Why? He is a Muslim. As it turns out, this has happened to many other prominent American Muslims. As reported in 2011, the FBI teaches its operatives that 'mainstream Muslims' are 'violent, radical'.[2] Faisal Gill's story is just one of many that has come to light thanks to Snowden. It raises questions about how these things happen – the Foreign Intelligence Surveillance Act was supposed to limit McCarthy-like witch-hunt excesses after 9/11 – about access to electronic communication, including emails and social media, by police, security and intelligence agencies. It also throws down a gauntlet about privacy rights, democracy and dignity.

This case is important because it shows that not only is Faisal Gill susceptible to surveillance, like anyone else within sight of the NSA, but he is also in a group singled out for special scrutiny, as an American Muslim. Thus his rights to privacy have not only been diminished along with millions of others, but they are, apparently, different from those in other groups. He was deeply disturbed to discover that he was being surveilled because he is fully aware that part of what it means to live in a democracy is to know what the government is doing and to have the chance to question it, if necessary.

The word privacy appears with great frequency among those who question the appropriateness of what the NSA and its partners do. Privacy unites a variety of oppositional figures of all political stripes in a post-Snowden world. This chapter explores what is meant by privacy and why it is indispensable. Privacy is a pivotal concept that helps to throw light on what is wrong with mass surveillance and there are many levels on which it can be used for this purpose. Privacy is also closely connected with other categories of complaint against mass surveillance, including rights such as freedom of association, speech, religion, conscience, movement – rights that are basic to democratic ways of organizing society.

Snowden's own comments certainly point to privacy as a vital value and one that should be maintained by more than one means. Speaking in June 2014 on the first anniversary of the initial leaks, for example, he said that users should seize privacy, 'take back the net', by adopting encryption for their computers and digital devices. But he also argued for using political means – voting for those who would limit unnecessary and illegal surveillance, as a way of combating mass surveillance of the kind that his work has revealed.[3] More broadly still, he often speaks of the need to eliminate mass surveillance as something that is incompatible with democratic practices. In this broader sweep, there are cases such as that of Faisal Gill. Post-Snowden politics also speaks to his situation. How do we square specific surveillance of Gill and his family, simply because they are Muslim, with living in a fair and just society?

This chapter starts out with privacy as conventionally construed, and then moves out to think of privacy in several different dimensions. The chapter concludes by discussing the extent to which mass surveillance should even be contemplated in societies that lay claim to being democratic. The twist in the tail is the question of whether societies that permit mass surveillance and put pressure on privacy are actually undermining the very possibility of politics.

Privacy Asserted: The Back-Story

Wherever there is pervasive state-initiated surveillance, the same questions have to be asked. Privacy is under threat in new ways. How this is perceived varies from country to country but most agree that there is personal and social benefit from having a realm where people can think, write, talk, play or generally 'be themselves' away from the eyes and ears of others, especially those in authority. Privacy is often seen as having a number of dimensions: the choice to be let alone – 'unhindered', that is – limiting others' access to the self, and rights to secrecy, control of personal information, personhood and intimacy.[4] But these interpretations vary widely, especially beyond Western countries that often seem to focus on individual rather than collective values.

Privacy is generally regarded as a 'right' or a 'civil liberty' associated with being a free person. The UN High Commissioner for Human Rights reminded us in 2014, for example, that 'surveillance threatens individual rights – including to privacy and to freedom of expression and association – and inhibits the free functioning of a vibrant civil society'.[5] The attacks of 9/11 provoked much interest in privacy around the world after national security policies were enacted that frequently infringed 'informational privacy'. Personal data were crossing borders faster, more frequently, and with fewer controls than before. A key problem is that, typically, information privacy is often seen in law as less important than bodily or territorial privacy.

Yet, as the Snowden revelations show, facial images (body) or location data (territory) are often collapsed into a more bland general category of information relating to persons or groups. Privacy is also connected with living in a democratic society, where there are statutory limits to what government may do secretly, and where we should be able to disagree with the government without fearing the consequences. Why should any democratic government record someone's opposition to anything from abortion and euthanasia to oil pipelines, factory farms or mines run from abroad and supported by foreign governments?

Why are privacy rights and democracy challenged by surveillance today? Both have been achieved only through long struggle and both are fragile and vulnerable. Like beautiful pottery, these things are easier to break than to mend. So how exactly does the surveillance which has been revealed threaten to crack open or break up privacy rights and democracy? And can we even talk about these in the same way in a digital, 'big data' era? In the northern hemisphere, with ripple effects around the world, 9/11 unleashed many challenges to privacy.[6] The anti-terrorist laws that permitted this were – sometimes – publicly debated, but the agencies that carried them out tend to be highly secretive. The Snowden revelations show just what kinds of things happen behind the closed and heavily guarded doors of the NSA and similar organizations.

We have known since the 1960s about the tendency of police departments in North America, Europe and elsewhere to keep more and more population groups under surveillance, and since the 1970s that, in the name of national security, intelligence and communications agencies were doing the same.[7] Since the 1980s a number of researchers have shown that this trend has been massively amplified by computerization.[8] Note three things:

One, information and risk are central: By the 1990s policing and security was increasingly *defined* in terms of information-handling and its rationale was to manage risks.[9] So the threats to privacy, rights and democracy after 9/11 came as no surprise, although public opposition to these trends never seemed strong or sustained, at least in North America. With the Snowden disclosures, a new and dramatic opportunity to respond to these challenges is presented. The evidence of international mass surveillance of the everyday lives of ordinary citizens grows with each new revelation.

Two, everyone is targeted: It is now widely known that mass surveillance means that 'innocent bystanders' are included in the NSA's surveillance net, both Americans and citizens of many other countries – nine out of ten NSA communications touch innocent people like these.[10] The colossal collection, storage and analysis of personal data – much of which seems trivial, fragmented, inconsequential – from numerous sources is much more difficult to pin down or even

to see as an issue. In fact, as we have seen, privacy is everyone's problem.

Three, individuals are 'made up': Mass surveillance uses
data in new ways that disconnect the data from the individual
– I call it 'personal data without the person' – but the profiles
created from such data gathering are often misleading, irrelevant and damaging to specific individuals or groups. The
ways in which people are 'made up' by the data in these
impersonal systems are far from incidental in the real flesh-
and-blood lives of those people.

Privacy Versus Surveillance

Privacy then, is a vital part of the Snowden story. Glenn
Greenwald, for example, points out that when government
or business says privacy is less important today, individual
spokespersons do not believe what they themselves say. In
the US, when Senator Dianne Feinstein asserted the NSA's
collection of metadata is not surveillance, online protesters
demanded that she publish a monthly list of people she called
and emailed, with details of where she was and how long she
was in touch. It was inconceivable that she would agree, says
Greenwald, because it was a 'clear breach of the private
realm'.[11] True enough.

This is typical of the way that the concept of privacy is
invoked as an antidote to surveillance. The concept is made
to do much work – often with considerable success – in
mobilizing the assessment of, and limits to, surveillance. But
in order to explore privacy as a means of resisting increasing
government surveillance – especially mass surveillance –
much more has to be considered than what Senator Feinstein
might not want to be revealed in a public inventory of her
email and phone communications and personal itinerary, as

Greenwald would be the first to agree. The Snowden revelations are about government surveillance of ordinary citizens, often in the name of national security, that goes well beyond the generally accepted targeted monitoring of those whom policing and intelligence agencies have reason to believe are a direct threat.

Snowden has pulled back the curtain on some huge surveillance secrets. Telephone and internet companies are implicated. The Dishfire program makes it possible for the NSA to scan 200 million text messages of US citizens each day. The NSA spies on world leaders – 122 of them according to *Der Spiegel* – often using their cellphones. It also intercepts phone calls across whole countries, such as Afghanistan, using a program called Mystic to 'replay' conversations from the past.[12] The NSA weakens the security of the internet by cracking or circumventing attempts at encryption. The NSA's TAO – Tailored Access Operations – hacks the internet worldwide and injects malware into the system.[13]

Hardly surprising that 'privacy' appears with such frequency in outraged denunciations of the NSA. Citizens of not only the US but also of many other countries around the world know that their private calls, texts, internet surfing and emails are subject to scrutiny by the NSA and its partners. But the debates occur differently in different countries and opinion polls show considerable variations in public views of what privacy is, why it might be important and whether it may have to be 'traded' for more security at certain times of crisis. With the rise of social media, a further question is added to the mix: does privacy really matter any more when all kinds of personal information and images are voluntarily shared online? Knowing what is meant by privacy is vital if we are to work out what the appropriate responses to Snowden's revelations are.

For example, an international poll taken in 2014 showed that, around the world, 64 per cent of respondents are more concerned about online privacy than in 2013.[14] At 46 per cent Sweden had the lowest rise in the rate of concern about privacy since Snowden's revelations, compared with 62 per cent in the United States. Increased concern about privacy was much more marked in Brazil, India and Nigeria, which each registered at 83 per cent. Although Americans also worry about the security of their information on the internet (only 31 per cent said it is secure), only 36 per cent have done anything to improve their privacy, compared to 69 per cent of Indian respondents.

Such international variations are important, reflecting different levels of dependence on the internet, among other things. While 77 per cent of Americans think that access to the internet is a basic human right, more than 90 per cent of respondents from China, Egypt, Indonesia, Nigeria and Tunisia say so. However widespread the agreement that much is wrong with the way that the NSA operates – this would be one good explanation of the increased concern about privacy – responses to privacy issues vary considerably around the world. And even when people say that they are concerned they do not necessarily attempt to do anything about it.

Why Privacy Matters

Privacy matters both as a vital value in itself and also for other practices that it supports – such as democracy. It is a robust way of questioning the growth of surveillance, and is undoubtedly the most widely used platform for mobilizing opposition to unnecessary and especially mass surveillance. The fact that it can all too easily be reduced to an individualistic level by both its supporters *and* its detractors is not an argument for abandoning it. It is rather a challenge to show in what ways privacy is a social and a public good. Nor is the fact that it is historically and culturally relative, or that some languages, such as Japanese or even French, have no single word that corresponds to the English 'privacy', sufficient reason for dropping the term. To the contrary, it is a reason for showing how context is always crucial. 'Privacy' does not speak equally clearly to all aspects of what is wrong with some forms of surveillance. But this is an argument for finding supplementary ways of querying surveillance, not for letting go of privacy.

Space does not permit a full discussion of these matters, especially the critique of inadequate ways of defining privacy.[15] As one who was once known for some fairly severe strictures against privacy, I should say that over the past decade two things have influenced my altered position. One is that as surveillance issues have become more urgent, the need to find common ground for opposition to its negative features has become a priority. And the other is that definitions of privacy are turning from abstract, individualistic and sometimes elitist emphases to much more welcome ones that accent our everyday embodied lives in their relational dimensions. Privacy is part of the common good.

Firstly, privacy is a matter of public policy and, as such, is now often couched in terms of its social and societal benefits, on both sides of the Atlantic and beyond. Most privacy and data protection laws were created precisely because computerization increasingly meant that issues of personal information-handling could not be limited to extraordinary or occasional events. People using credit cards or social insurance numbers in the first instance, and then anyone using digital devices, were more and more vulnerable to system errors, fraud, security breaches – or to direct unauthorized or secondary use of their personal data. Privacy policy speaks to these matters of public importance – all the more so when the surveillance is done by government agencies like the NSA and its partners without specific warrant and with little or nothing by way of transparency or accountability.

Secondly, privacy never exists in a vacuum. Context makes a difference to what is considered private and this has never been more true than in a day of widespread online communications. The mere fact that many social media users post freely and frequently does not necessarily indicate a lack of interest in privacy so much as a nuanced understanding of what should be confidential or anonymous or protected in varying settings. Young people in Canada, for example, are very clear about the need for limits to the circulation of their posts and, especially, their photos. And while they might think that under some circumstances the police should be allowed to gain access to their data, others, such as teachers, should certainly not be able to see their social media pages.[17] What this means is that privacy regulation should be flexible enough to address such variations while still remaining clear that certain kinds of surveillance are simply unacceptable.[18]

Thirdly, while privacy may not address all aspects of surveillance, privacy policies are constantly being developed to try to ensure that they remain relevant. For example, privacy may be inadequately construed as creating a bubble around the individual, a barrier that should not be transgressed. But as political scientist Colin Bennett points out, most privacy thinkers and policy-makers today recognize that we all *already have* extensive relationships with organizations that handle personal data.

So the question is not so much about privacy as some line in the sand, but rather how those relationships are managed and the extent to which we can trust organizations to take every care of the data while they are in their systems.[19] Which was exactly what prompted such a scandal when Snowden revealed that phone and internet companies were working with the NSA. Trust between individuals and organizations is fractured when information collected for one purpose and supposedly protected from prying eyes is in fact in use by another, secretive and less than accountable agency.

To take Bennett's argument one stage further, the key reason for seeing privacy as an important value is that it sees human beings as relational. Privacy thought of in individualist terms falls woefully short. Being relational is basic to being human.[29] As Catherine Fieschi says, for humans to thrive, their 'interdependence entailing knowledge of each other and various forms of trust' are essential.[21] German sociologist Georg Simmel pointed out – at the start of the twentieth century – that how we relate to others depends deeply on what we know, and do not know, about them.[22] In this case, too, privacy is connected with an ethics of care for the other. Interdependence and trust assumes care.

In short, privacy as a value is essential. More may be needed but not less than privacy. The concept does mobilize regulation and action and contributes to the common good. Privacy is an essential component of democracy and of a decent human life. At times it has been narrowly conceived as an abstract disembodied ideal, which fails to do justice to the real-life situations to which it in fact refers.[23] It has been criticized for emphasizing the spatial dimension and neglecting social justice aspects of surveillance such as social sorting. Fault has been found when it is reduced to 'information control' rather than being seen in a broader context of rights. It is historically and culturally relative. And today, the concept is also changing in a digital era, which raises further questions about how to retain its effectiveness. But in no way do these things simply or completely add up to a case against privacy.

Privacy is thus the right place to start, simply because in its emerging form it has the capacity to frame opposition to excessive or unwarranted surveillance. Debates over privacy, in this view, foster political, policy and practical change. As privacy expert Valerie Steeves says, 'narrower conceptions of privacy are being displaced by more empowering discourses from a human rights model that protects human dignity and democratic freedoms'.[24] It is vital to work with those who take this view[25] because they are fully aware of the need both to limit surveillance and to work within the parameters of a concept – privacy – that has served that end in public policy for many decades.

Whistleblowers, Journalists and Other Targets

Some Snowden documents released early in 2015 show that emails from journalists from the BBC, Reuters, *The Guardian*, the *New York Times*, *Le Monde*, *The Sun*, NBC and the *Washington Post* were scooped up in 2008 by GCHQ.[26] Apparently a new tool for stripping irrelevant material from emails was under test. Documents also draw attention to the fact that investigative journalists are seen as a threat alongside terrorists and hackers. One restricted document intended for army intelligence officials observes that 'journalists and reporters representing all types of news media represent a potential threat to security'.

In the UK, more than a hundred editors of newspapers and other news media signed a letter to Prime Minister David Cameron protesting this snooping on journalists' communications.[27] More general opposition to NSA interception and analysis of journalists' and others' communications has occurred in various places in Europe and the US – such as 'Restore the Fourth', meaning the Fourth

Amendment of the American Constitution, on the annual Fourth of July Independence Day. Such resistance to the curtailing of civil liberties makes sense, given the direct challenge to human rights. A democracy depends directly on a free press.

An important outcome of the Snowden revelations was to prompt President Obama to commission a report by the President's Review Group on Intelligence and Communications Technologies, published as *The NSA Report: Liberty and Security in a Changing World* (2014).[28] Significantly, this report speaks of both privacy and civil liberties, which connects directly with human rights. The authors are clear that 'the current storage by the government of bulk metadata creates potential risks to public trust, personal privacy and civil liberty'.[29] They explicitly state that the rights to freedom and civil liberties that may be threatened online go well beyond privacy. As we have seen, post-Snowden calls for human rights have also been heard in the UN General Assembly, in a speech given in 2013 by Brazilian President Dilma Rousseff.

So privacy itself may be thought of as a right, but other rights – to speak out, to dissent, even to dig below the surface as a reporter – may also be at issue when one is fearful that conversations are being monitored by the NSA or any other agency. Article 12 of the Universal Declaration of Human Rights asserts that our reputation should not be impugned, our homes entered or our correspondence intercepted without good reason.

On 16 July 2014 the UN High Commissioner for Human Rights spoke out against the 'disturbing lack of transparency about government surveillance...' that causes human rights violations.[30] But article 19 of the Universal Declaration also speaks to the Snowden affair: the right to freedom of expression. Free speech is also jeopardized by mass surveillance.

Privacy is for all. But the other rights at stake give even more reasons for opposing excessive, unwarranted and illegal surveillance. And seeking privacy as a right may help to bolster those rights as well.

Over the past two decades, it has become increasingly clear that surveillance is unevenly distributed. That is, some population groups find themselves under more intensive scrutiny than others, or because the data are processed in particular ways, some groups are unjustly discriminated against. Since 9/11, for example, airport security checks in North America, Europe and elsewhere have resulted in disproportionate delays and detainment for brown-skinned people, especially if they appear to have 'Muslim' or 'Arab' features or profiles. Recall the Faisal Gill example. As well, already marginalized groups such as African Americans in the US, refugees from the global south in Europe, or the poor – anywhere – also find that they are singled out for further disadvantage whether through the surveillance mechanisms of welfare or credit-ratings.[31]

The Snowden revelations themselves show the extent of government attempts to stifle popular protest and political dissent. I noted earlier the collaboration between the Canadian CSE and the NSA to monitor the G8 and G20 meetings in 2010. The secret surveillance of the summit meetings included scanning for possible 'troublemakers' who might be making their way to Toronto by rail or road and whose activities could be tracked as they arrived. An 'internet monitoring unit' was deployed by the Royal Canadian Mounted Police (the federal police), for instance, although it is hard to discover exactly how this worked. Equally, how judgements were made about the identity of 'troublemakers' is unclear. What is clear, however, is that more carefully restricted surveillance practices would help to prevent the predictable scenes that ensued.[32]

The protests at the G20 in Toronto were notorious for the TV images of gratuitous street violence by some, and also by police – leading to calls for a public inquiry from Amnesty International and complaints about brutality from well-respected figures.[33] A student friend of mine attending a prayer vigil at the protests was arrested and fined heavily on the grounds that the pocket knife he carried in his backpack to cut fruit for the group was a 'dangerous weapon'. The aim of the authorities was clearly to intimidate any who wished to express their views – whether to God or to fellow citizens – publicly.

So it is vital to pursue a rights-based approach to surveillance that acknowledges privacy as a value to be maintained for all, but also one to be stressed in relation to those who face unfair discrimination through the targeting of 'suspect' groups – the social sorting of surveillance. Privacy is a springboard into these broader issues. Rights-based approaches are important and belong alongside others, such as a critical ethics of care.[34] If there are rights to fair treatment, there are also rights to express oneself, even to go out on a limb if the situation calls for it. The question of protest, dissent and whistleblowing raises further issues, that also prompt questions about surveillance and democracy.

Since Snowden, it has become even more apparent in many countries that dissenters, protesters, whistleblowers and indeed anyone who criticizes government and corporate power is likely to come under special scrutiny. Snowden himself provides a case in point. It was only after he could find no internal support for his complaints about illegal practices within the NSA that he decided on civil disobedience. Seeing the attacks on and accusations against other whistleblowers in the US – from Daniel Ellsberg of Pentagon Papers fame, to William Binney or Thomas Drake, who also exposed NSA activities – he chose to share his

findings with journalists and to seek safe haven outside
the US.

Snowden chose not to speak out as a whistleblower
and allow the news to be picked up by the media. Instead,
he contacted filmmaker Laura Poitras and investigative
journalist Glenn Greenwald and invited them to participate
in the process. Journalists were thus involved and in a
sense implicated in the revelations. *The Guardian* (UK)
and the *Washington Post* (US) actually broke the news but
other papers, including the *South China Morning Post*
(Hong Kong), *Der Spiegel* (Germany), *O Globo* (Brazil),
L'Espresso (Italy) and the *New York Times* (US), have also
played a role.

However, elements in the mass media also succeeded in
casting slurs on Snowden from the start, smearing him as a
traitor or worse. The government clampdown on the press
that often keeps ordinary citizens from full awareness of
other important news worked overtime to dismiss Snowden
or deflect attention from the significance of his act. Even the
New York Times, which seemed fairly even-handed in its
Snowden coverage, took until New Year's Day 2014 to declare
that 'whistleblower' is the correct descriptor for him and to
state unequivocally that he should be given the 'hope of a life
advocating for privacy and far stronger oversight of the
runaway intelligence community'.[35]

Several other aspects of this should be highlighted. The
fear of retaliation in a world of information control is strong.
Increased government surveillance may at certain times
create chilling effects and self-censorship. A striking instance
of this appeared in a survey of American writers by PEN in
2013 that showed how, following the Snowden disclosures,
one in six authors were limiting what they said or avoiding
certain topics for fear of reprisals.[36] Such chilling effects are
a serious matter when it comes to civil liberties and human

rights. They may not sound very tangible but they are all too real in their consequences.

Paralleling this, a Pew Internet and American Life study in 2014 showed that many in the US were withdrawing from using social media to discuss the Snowden findings. Only 42 per cent of those polled would risk such a discussion, compared with 86 per cent who would consider talking about mass surveillance offline. And even those social media users who might discuss Snowden with friends, face-to-face, were less likely than non-social media users to do so. This may reflect the fact that Facebook was one of the companies named within the post-Snowden debate, but nonetheless it at least suggests that social media are not necessarily a space where users feel freer than in offline relationships to discuss matters like this.[37]

What this shows, rather starkly, is that in the aftermath of the Snowden revelations, the choice of supposed security is very much at the expense of liberty. People are increasingly suspicious and wary. The spectre of fear is abroad, fostered by governments reacting hastily and ill-advisedly to attacks that may be described as 'terrorist' ones, and further amplified by mass media. This is deeply destructive of trust and care. How can cooperation, so vital to any democracy, develop when it is stretched to tearing point by uncertainty and distrust? If we are scared to speak or write about certain topics, democracy, dignity and political debate stand little chance.

Democracy and Surveillance: Security Trumps Politics

Can mass surveillance ever be consistent with democracy? It is fair to say that surveillance and democracy have an unsettled and tense relationship. Surveillance can curb freedoms, inhibit democracy and, at worst, lead to totalitarianism – as

George Orwell and Hannah Arendt famously feared. For Arendt, a political theorist who shone a light on totalitarianism in the 1950s and 1960s, signs that the state was tightening its grip included naming 'objective opponents', who changed depending on the circumstances, and having secret policing agencies – a 'state within the state' – whose task was 'not to discover crimes, but to be on guard when the government decides to arrest a certain category of the population'.[38] Do these not ring bells as we confront the realities revealed by Snowden?

For those who work within surveillance agencies, however, recognizing this may be extremely difficult. Snowden himself speaks of the everyday routines that make operatives case-hardened within institutions like the NSA. Surveillance is what they do at their desks, manipulating the data on their computer screens. It is easy for them to lose sight of the life-altering and invasive ways that surveillance can impact people's prospects. Tens of thousands of employees work in these agencies in the US alone and the growth of intelligence services since 9/11 has been huge.[39] No wonder Arendt, speaking of a quite different context and time, noted that apparently humane citizens could, when they worked in their official bureaucratic capacity, unwittingly help the Holocaust to happen. She called it the 'banality of evil'.[40]

But what is democracy? Power exercised by people? Open procedures with equal rights to speak? Struggling to keep the public domain public?[41] Many would argue that democracy can contribute to effective decision-making and protect from corruptions of power.[42] Key aspects of democracy that have a bearing on surveillance include the accountability of government to its citizens. This means that citizens need access to information and a free press to assess government. Civil liberties and human rights protect these. The problem is that in the twenty-first century the world has moved on from when Orwell and Arendt were its critics. The state is all too often a *corporate* state that pays lip-service to democratic ideals and simultaneously makes authentic participation very difficult.[43] And it has built a surveillance engine, as revealed by Snowden, that is having negative – and potentially devastating – effects on democracy.

As previously stated, surveillance is monitoring for intervention. Mushrooming surveillance alters the dynamics of visibility. Yet today, surveillance is normalized in the routines of everyday life, with worries only about its 'excesses'. Generally, the growth of surveillance seems to be seen more as necessary than negative. Few appear to see mass surveillance as a danger for democracy, eroding democratic institutions and public trust. It is true, of course, that in some respects democracy depends on surveillance. The same list of citizens that ensures 'one person one vote' may also be used to augment state power. Voter lists and registration may have positive effects in increasing development in contemporary as well as in historical societies.[44] Such ambiguities are ever-present and complicate simple stories of surveillance. But they never make surveillance neutral. They should not distract us from the stark realities of the apparently uncontrolled surveillance currently corroding the basic structural supports of democracy.

As well, equal citizenship may be eroded by categorical sorting, targeted voter systems and the like, each of which is surveillance-enabled. Even information narrowcasting on the internet, based on 'customized' contact, depends on personal data analysis. It creates what internet commentator Eli Pariser calls 'filter bubbles', in which people find their views reinforced through an echo-chamber of 'personalization' rather than engaging in broader debate.[45] This can produce less interest in the outlook and practices of others. One could be forgiven for thinking that such filter bubbles already play a key role in distracting attention from looming issues like mass surveillance and creating a narrowly informed or passive citizenry.

Some worry, beyond this, that in post-Snowden times we may move away from both democracy and politics itself. Since 9/11 it has become clear that security trumps politics. A perceived crisis gave birth to emergency measures; exceptional circumstances demanded immediate, visible and appropriate action. The problem, as Italian philosopher Giorgio Agamben reminds us, is that while such 'states of exception' – where law is temporarily suspended for the public good – may be needed in the heat of the moment, they are meant to be short-lived, limited. But now classified 'reasons of state' make them permanent. Two things happen, or rather, do not happen: security remains ill-defined and no formal state of exception is declared.[46]

Firstly, security is paraded as a priority but what security actually entails remains cloudy. It seems amazing that the 'security' slogan that has dominated global politics as well as many realities of everyday life for more than a decade lacks clear definition. It is of course used in very different ways in different contexts. The idea that aiding the escape from poverty could be construed as a quest for security has been displaced by security as the control of terrorism in many countries of the global north but not, until recently, in the global south.[47]

As Lucia Zedner, professor of criminology, dramatically notes, security has the qualities of an errant fire truck. It is permitted to drive through city streets with lights flashing and sirens blaring even at risk of harming other road users. She wisely continues, 'The pursuit of security signals an urgency and importance that stifles debates as to priorities, resources and countervailing interests. To invoke security is to move to foreclose debate as to the wisdom of a policy or the necessity of a measure.'[48] Security becomes of the utmost importance.

Thankfully, this is recognized in some important post-Snowden documents, such as the American *NSA Report*. The authors make it quite clear that security should be attached with equal strength to the words 'national' and 'personal'.[49] The latter includes, they say, Fourth Amendment rights to be 'secure in their persons, houses, papers, and effects, against unreasonable searches and seizures...' They also reject outright the insidious view that a 'balance' must be sought between these two understandings of security. 'In a free society,' they assert, 'public officials should never engage in surveillance to punish their political enemies; to restrict freedom of speech or religion; to suppress legitimate criticism or dissent; to help their preferred companies or industries...' and so on.[50] But will these words be heeded?

The frequency with which one hears of the 'balance' or 'trade-off' between privacy and security, or liberty and security, is matched only by its hollowness. Some legal experts love this. They hold 'threats' in one hand and 'individual harms' in the other, frequently forgetting that privacy is about relationships and the common good. 'Balance' really means nothing but it does lend spurious weight to the claim that rights to privacy, freedom of speech or whatever have to be curtailed in the quest for a greater good of a vague and undefined national security. Many have rejected the false splitting of 'national' and 'personal' concerns but as yet, alas, to no avail, at least in public attitudes.[51] Yet the only way to restore the public's frayed confidence in intelligence agencies and indeed in Western governments in general – as far as the shibboleth of security is concerned – is both to define terms clearly and to be transparent about how goals in each area are being sought.

Secondly, the lack of any formal declaration of a state of exception emerges from a steady but secretive process of changing the rules for dealing with crime. There is a marked shift from trying to understand *causes*, to managing *effects*. Crime control generally has shifted since the later twentieth century away from attempting to understand the environmental and social roots of certain types of crime and towards dealing with its impact.[52] This is why, for example, Prime Minister Stephen Harper of Canada cautions against 'committing sociology' when trying to understand the case of hundreds of missing and murdered Aboriginal women. Causes have to be known, effects call for control.

Agamben uses the example of biometrics, which were first used to check on previous offences and had no role in crime prevention. During the twentieth century, biometrics was increasingly applied to other areas of life, such that any and all citizens might be subject to biometric identification and authentication. Today this has expanded even further. We may use biometric controls to enter our offices or our cars, to cross borders, and even children may use them to purchase food in the school lunch break. Well beyond fingerprints, then, many biometric technologies have spread into numerous areas of everyday life, where a generalized control is evident – but often, no comment is made. It is taken for granted. Normal.

Modern dreams of citizenship seem rather detached from the passive citizenship of today. If Agamben is right in his fears about biometrics, it is not our place in the public sphere but our biological and now metadata that yields our 'identity'. Risk management approaches, dominant in the US and Europe since the 1980s, encourage officials to think that all citizens may be potential terrorists, and therefore control is clearly appropriate. Such modes of governance fit well with free market economics, because the right task of government is seen as controlling effects, not querying causes. Hence the enhanced policing becomes more and more militarized and information-intensive. And if we are all potential terrorists then the close attention by authorities paid to dissidents, protesters and whistleblowers makes sense. The active and adversarial citizens assumed by classic democratic theory are unwelcome today. All citizens are being reclassified as potential threats to state security.

Beyond Privacy?

The story of Faisal Gill demonstrates that much is at stake following the Snowden revelations. In particular, while privacy is tremendously valuable as a mobilizing slogan, it can easily be reduced to abstract matters with little connection to the real world. And it can be domesticated and used as a means of indicating that organizations are 'clean' – they can check the privacy boxes and continue their practices. Privacy, paradoxically, may enable surveillance. Alternatively, the kind of privacy that makes sense in post-Snowden times sees the common good as paramount, and cares deeply about protecting the other person, not merely about 'my privacy'.

Faisal Gill's story also shows how surveillance is a means of social sorting. In this case, the sorting negatively discriminates between different groups in the population so that one group can be treated differently from another. This example shows how easily a social category may be used to expand the range of a prejudicial conjunction of terms: 'Muslim' and 'security threat'. And it indicates how correct Snowden is to say that 'your rights matter because you never know when you may need them'. Faisal Gill imagined that, as a responsible citizen, he had nothing to hide or to fear. In fact, he was under constant surveillance simply because of his identification as a Muslim. Privacy connects here with religious freedom.

Snowden also asks what kind of world we want to live in? Is it one marked by fear and mutual suspicion, where data is collected promiscuously and kept forever, in systems that never forget, making forgiveness obsolete and creating much to fear even though you have nothing to hide? Is it one where vulnerability is amplified, democracy diminished and where ordinary people are more exposed to organizations that are themselves more opaque? Or is it a different kind of society, the contours of which we can imagine but not yet experience?

The issue of 'framing' really applies to the whole question of surveillance in the twenty-first century. How do we think about these large and looming questions? How important is internet privacy – and indeed the role of the world's nation-states in monitoring and tracking individuals using metadata? Should we ignore such matters, assuming that privacy is a thing of the past? Or should we shrink into a paranoid state, refusing to participate in the online world, trashing our smartphones and retreating into a realm of disconnection and dystopian fears? Or is there another way to approach the world that Snowden's stolen documents have revealed?

5

FRAMING FUTURES

Do we want to live in a controlled society or do we want to live in a free society? That's the fundamental question we're being faced with.

Edward Snowden, July 2014

On several occasions, Edward Snowden has observed that the world we have made is not merely 'Orwellian'. It is something much worse. And while his main focus is on the technological capacities that can easily turn an open internet into a cyber-cage, it is worth standing back to get a wider angle. Certainly, rampant mass surveillance is a deeply disturbing development and the NSA and its partners must become far more accountable and transparent if democratic rights are to be respected. But as we have seen, the internet as currently configured displays features that make it inherently surveillant, and this also goes for the whole 'networked society' and the global power flows that characterize it today. As Snowden says, 'a child born today will grow up with no conception of privacy at all – they will never know what it means to have a private moment to themselves, an unrecorded, unanalysed thought'.[1]

But who is listening to Snowden? His comments about children growing up without privacy does not seem to have much traction in this world that believes itself free of the Stasi of East Germany or the secret agents operating in Mao's China between 1949 and 1965.[2] Perhaps because of the dominance of consumerism, lulling us with the idea that freedom means 'free to choose' – in the mall – or maybe because memories have faded of McCarthyism and its surveillance-ridden witch-hunts, even the stark Snowden revelations do not yet seem able to jolt people into remedial action. Admittedly, it is hard to point to striking examples of who has become a damaged victim of NSA mass surveillance and the best we can do is to point to the expanded potential for political repression. The unspoken assumption is that 'it can't happen here!'

Yet as Chilean poet and academic Ariel Dorfman says, it was precisely that sentiment that gripped him and his compatriots in Chile before the brutal dictatorship that engulfed that country on 11 September 1973. They said 'it can't happen here!' In 2006 Dorfman visited the building of the Fundación Salvador Allende and was shown the tangled wires of the Pinochet surveillance centre, where those who spied on the civilian population did their work. It should not be forgotten that the US government created the conditions for that coup, just as they had done earlier in bringing down the government of democratically elected President Árbenz in Guatemala in 1954, and in other countries as well. In Guatemala City I have visited the grim Police National Archives where 80 million surveillance records were stored (and lay undiscovered until 2005) of police monitoring, torture and murder between 1961 and 1996, in the military dictatorship ushered in by the fall of Árbenz.[3] Some Guatemalans, too, did not believe such things could 'happen here'.

Dorfman expresses his astonishment that Americans – he has taught at Duke University for many years – can accept with such equanimity that surveillance comes, not from some 'furtive government program' but rather the records are 'incessantly culled and mined from consensual exchange – happily, voluntarily, loudly offered up to the blatant gods of commerce and the internet'.[4] As he says, the same people who fume about totalitarian meddling seem unaware that 'digital eyeballs are measuring and bundling and gouging their every action, every hit, every profile, every purchase, every trip, every medicine, every texting, every friending, every like, every smile, every frown'.

Clearly, Snowden himself is passionate about the risks of increased government surveillance by agencies such as the NSA. People who have lived through state surveillance of a directly damaging kind – where lives were at stake – scratch their heads, wondering why people would go along with this without complaint. They see Snowden's point. So, too, do members of minorities – especially Muslims in the countries of North America, Europe and elsewhere, since 9/11. Such people have learned to fear 'liberal democratic' governments, to alter their behaviour and to try to melt into the background. A Muslim man from western Canada says, 'Every time I enter the airport or get ready to travel, I do so with the caution of a criminal who is careful not to get caught; the only difference is – I am not a criminal!'[5] What happened to 'innocent until proven guilty'?

In this chapter, we turn to the question of how issues of surveillance – along with privacy, rights and democracy – are framed today. Why do we think about these things the way we do and why do we speak up about them or remain silent?

To understand this we have to look again at the powerful words that justify increased surveillance, among which 'security' is paramount. We have to look again at the context of faith-in-technology and the links between public-and-private that guide technical development and policy and the ways in which we are all implicated in this in everyday life.

In June 2013, when the first Snowden documents were released, sales of *Nineteen Eighty-Four* and Google searches for information about Orwell soared wildly.[6] It is hard to know if the author of the best-known surveillance dystopia ever would have been pleased or not. After all, Snowden observes that we should have heeded his warnings, to nip NSA mass surveillance in the bud, decades ago. Buying the book after the revelations have begun seems like a desperate and faintly futile measure. And in any case, as privacy expert Daniel Solove says, Orwell did not necessarily have the best metaphor for what we experience in the twenty-first century. What about Franz Kafka's novels about an inscrutable bureaucracy, where you are called by the police on charges that are not explained and you live a nightmare of uncertainty about who knows what about you and what the outcome will be? This is closer to the mark.[7]

But even Kafka does not capture the full sense of what is wrong with mass surveillance today. In a much more oblique style, Dave Eggers' ironic novel *The Circle* speaks more clearly to surveillance in the digital era.[8] The irony lies in the first line, where 24-year-old Mae lands a job at Silicon Valley's now-dominant company, known to all as the Circle: 'My God, thought Mae, this is heaven.' In glass-clad office spaces that enable all to be seen Mae is quickly equipped with one device after another to facilitate verbal and visual communication until almost nowhere remains secluded or sheltered from the eyes of others. The reader is led through Mae's multiple discoveries of what it means to be constantly visible to colleagues and to the corporation, how they justify the practice and what it does to relationships of all kinds. It is a cheerfully terrifying novel. In the end the novel is dystopian,[9] just as Orwell's and Kafka's are.

Part of the message of the present book is that while dystopias are important cautions, there is also scope for the utopian, emphatically not as a desperate drive to create the perfect society but as a means of imagining alternative futures. 'Utopian' in this sense is not an escapist and unrealistic world of fiction and fantasy but a hard-nosed confrontation with the conflicted realities of the present.

The kinds of conclusions that we have reached are not generally encouraging, to say the least. Security surveillance tends to breed unease and uncertainty as well as, for some, actual disadvantage and distress. Nor are these conclusions reassuring in terms of the ways that people's rights may easily be trampled, especially, as we have seen, if they are connected with already marginalized and vulnerable groups. As for the internet, born with such promise for increased open communication and democracy, much of the direction of the digital world seems to be the opposite of what early pioneers hoped for. Secrecy in powerful agencies and filter bubbles for end-users is not what they had in mind.

But that is to frame these developments in an entirely negative, dystopian way, to see only gloom and doom and only a politics of resistance. Why not reframe the debate by adding a politics of hope? We may not only note the consequences of and the efforts to restrain what is currently occurring with rampant mass surveillance but also state clearly what sort of world we *would* like to see. From the vantage point of such a vision, alternatives may more clearly be seen, discussed and, perhaps, implemented. In other words, while a wake-up call is entirely appropriate and necessary to indicate where today's surveillance trends are taking us, it is equally appropriate to propose a beckoning call that suggests how we can frame some alternatives. This requires that we accent the ethical dimension of our analysis.

Framing the Bad News

Years ago, the Surveillance Studies Centre in which I work set up its first dedicated website. We thought that it would enable us to stay in closer contact with other academic groups around the world who are interested in surveillance. We could compare notes more easily using our website. Then my colleague discovered that one could also track who had visited our site (this was more than a decade ago, remember) so we obtained a screenshot of who was checking us out. To our consternation, while we did find a few academics who were visiting the site, so also, prominently, were the Canadian Security Intelligence Service, the Royal Canadian Mounted Police and, yes, the Communications Security Establishment of Canada. Draw your own conclusions.

This book has surveyed some of the most striking implications of what, thanks to Snowden, we now know about 'national security' surveillance in the early twenty-first century. We have examined the historical question of why, when the surveillance society is already so well developed, Snowden's revelations were read in the media as a complete surprise. We have also addressed the current question about what the key aspects of today's surveillance are, how to understand them and what sorts of responses are appropriate. The future question, touched on here, considers what the internet has now come to signify, and how it might be reclaimed for its original promise, given that it is a key site for surveillance practices at several levels? And more broadly, of course, there is the looming future question of whether mass surveillance can be eliminated as an ethically inappropriate practice.

At the outset, however, we noted that the Snowden revelations raise questions about the very language commonly used to discuss the monitoring and tracking of daily life and responses to these practices: surveillance and privacy. Concepts are always contested, some more than others. And definitions are always difficult because they reveal the time, place and cultural assumptions of their origins. I have insisted that surveillance is never neutral. In some forms it has always been necessary as a way of monitoring situations for signs of danger or threat, a point that Snowden also makes. But even in its more benign forms it is not beyond ethics.

As with all practices, surveillance is subject to ethical assessment and can and should be contested. In other words, surveillance and its agencies may never be a law to themselves. Surveillance is a means to an end and those entrusted with surveillance tasks are answerable to those who define the ends. And I have argued that privacy, whatever its lingering limitations, remains a vital tool for questioning surveillance and for confronting surveillance with the lived realities of life. When seen alongside rights and democratic practices, privacy does point to alternatives.

Again, these questions have been raised before, but perhaps never so sharply as in relation to the post-Snowden scene. Once, the distinction between targeted and mass surveillance seemed fairly clear. No more. The lines blur with traffic between the two: is the person or the profile being surveilled? But in order to assess contemporary surveillance, the question still has to be asked – when is mass surveillance ever justified? The fact that the tools for mass surveillance are available in no way means that they have to be used. Once, privacy was construed primarily as a matter relating to the interests, or rights, of a specific identifiable individual. No

more. When profiling is 'anticipatory' and hunches about a
possible 'terrorist nexus' are the basis of suspicion, some ask
how exactly privacy addresses this? The difficulty here is that
privacy should be brought into play much earlier, to ask
about the acceptability of anticipatory profiling in the first
place. [9]

As we have seen, the kinds of surveillance highlighted by
the Snowden revelations are on the one hand information-
intensive, often relating to the internet, and on the other,
oriented to 'national security'. The previous chapter insists
that the concept of 'security' also requires some serious over-
haul in this context. As with surveillance or privacy, defining
security is difficult, especially under present conditions where
'national' security has been elevated to a top priority by many
governments. It is a highly contested concept, often construed as being in conflict with claims to a right to privacy
or to civil liberties.[10] Much more nuanced understandings of
security are required if the term is to retain any connection
with the desires, aspirations and indeed well-being of everyday citizens. And these must be considered in relation to the
other concepts – surveillance and privacy – discussed here.

The Snowden stakes are many and varied and differ from
country to country. But this complexity should not obscure
the fact that in all cases those stakes are high. The revelations
challenge some taken-for-granted assumptions and expose
the real gaps in current knowledge. But this is not only a
matter for those engaged in studying surveillance and
privacy.[11] At issue, in particular, is the future of the internet
and of digital communications in general, including how
ordinary users engage with these media. This is of course a
huge challenge. But the stakes are even higher and they
include the very character and possibilities for politics,
democracy and social justice in a time of post-Orwellian mass
surveillance.

What Alternative Is There?

We need ethical tools for assessing surveillance, a broadened sense of why privacy matters and ways of translating these into political goals. And it is essential that we do this with a clear sense of what kind of world we are working towards. How do we get a sense of what a better world would look like?

When Snowden offers us the stark choice – 'a controlled world or a free world' – he is saying two things. One, that his disclosures show us how our world is increasingly subject to unwelcome and undemocratic control. But two, that this is not the end of the story. The contrasting world is in his word, 'free'. It is one thing to complain about or oppose surveillance that is negatively conceived. This is important, indeed, vital, as I have argued. But it is another to explore the preferred alternatives. Because most surveillance and thus control involves networked digital data, this does not mean that the internet itself needs to be dismantled. No, the possibilities for freedom must lie in a search for alternative ways of shaping and governing the internet, and of engaging with it on a daily basis.[12]

Chapter 3 considered the question of big data, understood in relation to the Snowden disclosures. We saw how it has generated unprecedented public interest in surveillance in many countries around the world. Many technical and legal responses have been made and civil society activity has been much in evidence. At every level, accountability has been demanded – and, where appropriate, the *abolition* of some programs – from the NSA and its cognate agencies. But less progress has been made on what might be called a broad ethical front. Yet the questions raised are profound ones for which there are no ready answers. An ethical turn becomes more urgent as a mode of *critique*. This is so at several levels, but particularly in the kinds of ways that Snowden himself indicates through his repeated questions about 'what kind of society do we want?'

Properly ethical practices seem in short supply but interest in them is growing.[13] Big data, to continue with this example, is currently dominated by commercial and government criteria and these are often met with technical demands (for better encryption for example) or legal demands (for legislation relevant to regulating today's technologies). Privacy advocates and internet activists also try to promote new political approaches to emergent tendencies such as big data. But a key reason why those commercial and government criteria are so intertwined with big data is the strong affinity between the two, particularly in relation to surveillance. Big data represents a confluence of commercial and government interests. National security is a business goal as much as a political one and there is a revolving door between the two in the world of surveillance practices.[14] This is a major trend that calls for new approaches.

Ethical practices are at a relative disadvantage for several other reasons as well. Not many ethicists spend time thinking about the complexities of the internet, social media or big data, and many of those at the forefront of the big data field seem to have little time for ethics except as a minor, residual concern.[15] The imperatives for big data approaches come from a belief in the immense power of technology – can Google really track and predict the spread of flu faster than centres for disease control?[16] – along with the capacity to analyse vast quantities of data at steadily shrinking unit costs. But just as in the Google flu example, questions must be asked about how good the surveillance data and the modes of analysis are? How data are generated and framed always has decisive effects on the final outcomes of analysis.

Inescapably, surveillance and privacy have politics. In a world that still tries to insist that technologies are 'neutral', potential problems will still suggest to some that what is needed is better technology. But the ethical and political issues do not go away so easily. Surveillance and privacy each have a strong bearing on rights and democracy and vice versa. Democracy and surveillance are always in tension.

It is true that George Orwell commented on the lack of a clear definition of democracy, and even on the fact that defining democracy is sometimes resisted. And his imaginative writing bequeathed some of the more striking and enduring images of surveillance: the use of technology, the persistent, nagging sense of uncertainty of being watched, the personification of the surveillance state in Big Brother.[17] Orwell also acknowledged that coercion was only part of the story. He showed that surveillance works when it is internalized by its subjects so that it becomes 'natural' in their social consciousness. But Orwell is not necessarily the greatest guide to the *politics* of surveillance. Under pressure, Winston finally caved in.

Not only this. The way Orwell sometimes wrote of the working-class 'proles' suggests passivity, apathy; 'people who have never learned to think', he called them. Hope shrivels under such judgements. Yet Orwell knew what it was to be under surveillance for 12 years (for his undercover research for *The Road to Wigan Pier*)[18] and it did not deter him from resistance through writing. And as literary scholar Raymond Williams observes, 'Under controls as pervasive and as cruel, many men and women have kept faith with each other, have kept their courage and in several cases against heavy odds have risen to try to destroy the system or to change it.'[19] Unfortunately, many post-Snowden accounts of surveillance, updated for digital times, for global conditions and for the blurring of old boundaries between public and private agencies, are also – not without cause – pessimistic about the possibilities for politics.

Once, surveillance was about specific suspects and targets. Now, in an era of mass surveillance, no one is exempt, no one can evade surveillance. It is thus a key question for democracy today. And democratic responses, never more so than since the Snowden revelations began, are multiplying. The Council of Europe and even the US President have made interventions. The PEN International petition from more than 550 writers in 80 countries made waves in 2013.[20] Civil liberties and human rights groups are involved around the world.

Clarifying the Vision: Democracy, Dignity

As yet, efforts to galvanize a politics of surveillance have been somewhat piecemeal and issue-oriented. However, many privacy advocates and anti-surveillance groups exist and increasingly they find themselves in fruitful coalitions with each other.[21] The opportunities for questioning surveillance are expanding even as frequent attempts are made to shut them down.

The use of digital technologies in a hybrid, government-and-market context encourages a shift in tense in surveillance: it becomes markedly future-oriented. In order to promote steady control, past records become less significant than what is going to happen next and especially what individuals and groups will do next. Today's popular big data approaches to surveillance focus on the future, especially on *pre-emptive* prediction.[22] This carries risks, especially for time-honoured practices such as the 'presumption of innocence'. When data analytics produces its 'suspects' there's an invidious tendency for them to be treated as guilty. Thus the future is controlled in advance. And it looks dark.

What might turn on the lights? Recently, Ruth Levitas revived H. G. Wells's 1906 proposal that 'the creation of Utopias – and their exhaustive criticism – is the proper and distinctive method of sociology'.[23] She sees this as a way to critically expose limits of current policy, to offer holistic, reflexive and democratic ways of thinking about possible futures, to consider human needs and flourishing, not so much as a goal but simply as a method. Can we consider how a utopian method might help us reframe the world of surveillance? We commented earlier on the ways that democratic freedoms and human dignity are at risk in a world of mass surveillance. How could this be overcome?

Let us start with democracy. Its various characteristics include limited government: circumscribed claims and restricted power. Democracy promotes values that transcend any regime or party and encourages the accountability of government to the electorate, the people. Democracy acknowledges that the state is distinct from other aspects of life that may have their own integrity. It is also pluralistic and progressive – the latter in the sense that it is open to the future, seeing other possibilities than only present conditions. Democracy encourages dissent and diversity and fosters trust, not suspicion and fear. It is about respect, fairness and a commitment to rights.

This is a crucial area. Privacy, rights, and the rule of law are in many ways up for grabs after Snowden. Conspiracy theorists have a field day, while others stress structural shifts as the cause of this slippage. But both agree that democracy in any sense is at risk. Many things have become fluid: personal data flow between companies and government departments, security agencies seem more significant than nation-states, physical infrastructure like fibre-optic cables are conduits of political power, public/private distinctions are blurred. The 'state' intervenes in civil society in new and complex ways and 'security', as already noted, is used in contrast with, rather than alongside, 'liberty'.

And dignity? Human dignity relates to what people are worth as human beings. When dignity is respected, then people are treated in a particular way, as having rights to be treated thus.[24] This is connected with the critical ethics of care, mentioned earlier.[25] Some things, such as treating innocent citizens as if they were guilty of some crime, are incompatible with treating them with dignity and thus contravene their rights. As we have seen, this is exactly what can happen when surveillance is used to try to pre-empt some activity; the presumption of innocence fades.

Some rights, of course, go beyond this, and help us think in terms of human needs, what would be good in our lives. Not being unwillingly exposed or made visible in ways that damage a reputation is part of this. Fairness of treatment with regard to access to things like food or education or healthcare also has to do with human dignity, because they contribute to human flourishing. These too may be denied – but also, potentially, assured – by today's social sorting surveillance techniques.

The two familiar ideas, or better, practices, of promoting democracy and dignity can inform our views and the politics of preferable alternatives to the world of today's secretive state-and-corporate mass surveillance. They remind us of where we would rather live and how we would like to be treated – and to treat others. And they have to be rethought in light of digital developments and of the newly apparent realities of political life.

The Snowden revelations make clear what millions of us around the world should have known a long time ago. Indeed, had we known, had there been less over-secretive activity in intelligence agencies, no doubt people would have tried to resist the trends and redirect the policies. But much of what is done and how it is done remains secret and one of the first tasks is to demand transparency where it should exist – in government and business practices.

The domain in which these debates are perhaps most critical, and where we badly need a new sense of the positive possibilities, is the internet. The potential for open communication and the free sharing of ideas that once animated the young internet is still available. Tragically, today's internet – where many people actually live their daily lives – has become the site of the most intensive commercial and state surveillance.

Experts interviewed for a 2014 Pew report, *Net Threats*, in a series on Digital Life in 2025, say there will be more surveillance and less trust online as governments crack down on online freedom.[26] Worse, instead of recognizing and reacting against this, many have become inured to it and even engage in superfluous and sometimes damaging surveillance themselves. But it is not too late to propose and struggle for alternatives. This is happening on an increasing scale and the Snowden disclosures have only added to the energy for change.

Attempting to protect privacy is pivotal. Understood as a human right, it underlies aspects of democratic polity, such as freedom of expression. Often understood in the post-Snowden era as relating to control of communications about oneself, it is clearly a threatened value and not merely a forlorn hope, or a stage through which we have now passed. In chapter 3, however, we argued that it is vital that an ethics of big data practices be found that deals with the problem of the increasing gap between data and individuals.[27] Privacy remains the pre-eminent mobilizing concept for opposition to inappropriate, disproportionate or illegal surveillance. So

the efforts of those who propose legal limits, such as the need
for warrants to collect certain kinds of information, or technical limits such as encryption or de-identification, or who
would reinfuse the concept of privacy with content appropriate to a big data world, are entirely worthwhile.

As we also saw in chapter 4, privacy is called upon as a
means of defending fair treatment in several contexts. The
concept of social sorting alerts us to a number of related
practices that produce uneven and unequal outcomes when
the supposedly neutral and illuminating techniques of big
data – especially predictive profiling – are applied to perceived social and political problems. The profiling of Faisal
Gill is one case we looked at, but there are many others.
People's life-chances and reputations are made vulnerable by
such surveillant profiling. Bringing an ethic of care to bear
on such situations shows the need to promote the primacy
of the well-being and the worth of such individuals, and of
the communities of which they are a part.

Surveillance as social sorting connects both with modern
bureaucratic practices and also, prompted by the security
slogan, with insurance logic. The latter sees security as
dependent on intelligence gathering, identification and tracking.[28] Its outcomes – amplified in big data contexts – are
above all the growth of categorical suspicion.[29] Faisal Gill is
a suspect just because he falls into the 'serious Muslim' category. Things go badly awry at this point. The time-honoured practice of the 'presumption of innocence' – you're not
guilty until proven so – is out the window.[30]

The logic of insurance goes one stage further when it asks
for pre-emptive predictions. Recall that big data fosters an
anticipatory, future-tense approach to surveillance. Again,
this is not a new development in surveillance. Risk management techniques in particular have encouraged such 'anticipatory governance' for several decades. But the availability

of big data techniques encourages an intensified future-orientation in practice. So the possibility that, because of an apparent connection between certain data fragments, someone may be thought likely to behave in negative ways that are not yet evident leads to some action. The data have effects; they propel action. All too easily they turn an ordinary law-abiding citizen into a terror suspect.[31]

Critically, certain time-honoured legal protections such as a presumption of innocence or proof beyond reasonable doubt are being eroded within a number of Western societies precisely due to the developing reliance on big-data-led beliefs that suspects can be isolated by category and algorithm. Even if one-time 'suspects' have their names cleared by judicial process, the fact that big data practices exemplified in the collect-it-all slogan include retaining data indefinitely, it can be hard for persons with a 'record' ever to make a fresh start. Forgiveness? Forget it.[32] Data in the Canadian Police Information Centre, for example, remain there permanently. And when police include mental health problems in their records these can lead to denial of entry to Canadians trying to cross the border into the US. Attempted suicide calls, for example, have been uploaded to international databases with just this outcome.[33]

Big data is not revolutionizing surveillance but it is certainly increasing the scale of surveillance and the likelihood that serious errors will be made in identifying people as security threats. Big data practices are skewing surveillance even more towards a reliance on technological 'solutions'. This privileges organizations, large and small, whether public or private, over individual citizens. And it reinforces the shift in emphasis towards control while relying increasingly on predictive analytics to second-guess motives and intentions to try to prevent violence. Unfortunately, little time seems to be spent, at present, teaching students who work on big data projects to consider the ethical dimensions of what they are doing. Privacy and civil liberties are all too often seen in such contexts as a nuisance that holds up research. To bring in such topics could be one way of changing the climate and reframing how big data analysis is done.[34]

Surveillance and Human Flourishing

Snowden's revelations have done sterling service in showing how far state-based surveillance extends. But his work also shows how much surveillance today depends on other things. On the one hand, it depends on big data practices and thus on large corporations and government agencies, working in tandem. But, on the other, Snowden's work – and the outraged responses to the revelations – show how surveillance connects directly with everyday practices of ordinary internet and cellphone users.

At the end of the day, it is those ordinary everyday relationships that make up people's lives – all of our lives. That is why we need to develop a sense of how those big concepts – democracy, dignity – touch the things that matter. It is important to attend to the desires and hopes expressed in ordinary life: Can I trust that provider? Are my details safe on that site? Will my minority status jeopardize my prospects? How we translate these into policy action, policy, technical specifications and mundane ways of living will be crucial in determining whether the kinds of activities discovered and leaked by Snowden will be allowed to grow, malignantly, or be shut down, reined in or redirected.

Can we imagine things being different? Political philosopher Charles Taylor speaks of the 'social imaginaries' by which we imagine the societies that we inhabit and sustain.[35] They are both factual and normative; they have an ethical dimension. They tell us what 'works for us' and how we would like things to be 'moving forward'. They remind us that for most people, the immediate, the existential, comes before the institutional. We have a sense of where we have come from, where we are now, and where we are heading. We are in process; becoming. 'Human being' is rather a passive way of seeing ourselves; 'human becoming' would be closer to the mark. And that 'becoming' is almost always with others, on whom we depend – and they on us. Human flourishing is a state of discovering fulfilment, but simultaneously of active hopefulness that situations can be improved.

Adverse circumstances, on the other hand, may jeopardize our sense of well-being, and not merely cramp our style but introduce anxiety or fear. Out-of-control surveillance has just these effects, even when no police state has as yet come into being. Unfortunately, social scientists – I work as a sociologist – speak all too often as spectators of the human condition and not as participants. As Andrew Sayer notes, this means that we sometimes fail to grasp what really matters to people, what it is like to be vulnerable, to suffer, to feel capable and so on.[36]

The window into the world of surveillance that Snowden has opened for us does not offer an exhilarating view of how good things are going to be from now on. It does not reassure us that we can trust others, particularly some who have been given the responsibility for handling personal information. It actually creates uncertainties, worries and sometimes anger about secrecy and a failure to take due care of things that are precious to us – in this case, our personal details.

The world of the internet and of surveillance has these effects but it does not have to. There are alternatives. But we need to be clear about them. It is important to articulate our feelings about what is wrong. But equally important to consider, argue for and even struggle for a different way. The alternatives may be sought at every level, and that includes everyday life.

Much is made, of course, about finding new ways to protect ourselves, using encryption and other security-enhancing devices. Details about these are readily available online and elsewhere. This sounds fine, except for three things: One, online security seems to be inherently and chronically unstable. Two, relatively few users of the internet and social media are in a really knowledgeable position to be able to take advantage of whatever means of enhancing security are available. Some cannot afford them. And three, seeking such fixes keeps us in the thrall of 'technical solutions' to what are really political, social and personal problems.

This is not an argument against privacy-by-default-and-design or against the ethical education of computer scientists and software developers. Nor is it a sideswipe against those who have the technical expertise to use security devices such as encryption to protect their systems. No, it simply acknowledges that this is not enough in a world where the vast majority of vulnerable users are at a technical disadvantage. And that the problems have to be faced in the realm where they emerge, as practical, policy and political issues.

At a macro level, the crucial issues are how to protect *all* users of new media and how to ensure that those charged with responsibility for surveillance in every context aim at transparency and accountability. These may be thought of in terms of legal change and technological change – and at best, knowledgeable combinations of the two. Law cannot solve the problems, any more than technology can, but there are important initiatives that deserve support.

Some are spelled out, for instance, in the recommendations of *The NSA Report*, which stresses the link between privacy, human rights and democracy, and insists that the internet must be secure and open. Like other similar ones, this document is a starting point. It anticipates that others will take up the baton. Its authors wisely say that public trust is essential and that it is up to corporate and government bodies to prove that they are worthy of it. Their emphasis on *human* rights is shown, for instance, in their insistence that the privacy and dignity of citizens of other nations should be protected, inside and outside the US. Along with resolutions from the UN, referred to earlier, and in Europe, such initiatives at least throw some light into rather dark places.

At a micro level, too, the need to protect others and to be transparent and accountable is also vital. Surveillance affects everyone and there are ways in which we all participate in surveillance, wittingly or otherwise. Surveillance has become part of our own social imaginaries, contributing to surveillance culture, whether we like it or not. So to argue that large corporations or government agencies should become more transparent, accountable and responsible for protection without acknowledging that we too have to make changes could be read as having double standards. True, our lives are transparent to large organizations as never before, but many people work for organizations where they can actually make a difference at a local level.

This is the other side of the coin of demanding more democratic – transparent and accountable – practices of large corporate and government bodies. The challenge of the Snowden revelations is to all of us, globally and at every level. If we expect large agencies to be far more answerable for how they handle personal data, we can hardly have lower expectations of ourselves. Democratic participation affects every community, every institution. And everywhere, data – especially personal data – circulate more and more freely for multiple purposes.

So just as the revelations point not only to obviously macro-level demands such as greater government transparency and accountability, they also throw light on the micro-level use of everyday metadata, so we need to be more aware in everyday life of the issues surrounding ubiquitous data. We all have opportunities to minimize data or to be careful with how information about others, and of course ourselves, is used, in our social media worlds, our offices, our communities. We can democratize our own organizations and practices, on whatever scale.

This is a further reason for urging a reframing of surveillance and privacy today. The worst-case scenarios certainly give us pause, especially when we recall how people just like us confidently said 'it can't happen here'. It can and, unstopped, will happen here, wherever 'here' is. But the imaginary *reconstitution* of society, where we pause to consider what kind of a digital, communicative world we *do* desire, places the surveillance-intensive society revealed by Snowden in a starkly unfavourable light.

In such an imaginative exercise, it is our ordinary, everyday relationships – not the machinations of global power elites – that are primarily in view. These foster a right sense of priorities that produce both indignation that things should have been allowed to develop so very far *and* a determination not to allow them to develop further.

When Snowden asks whether we want to live in a 'controlled society' or a 'free society' he is asking us to attend to the larger frame, to be aware of the basic ethical questions and choices that confront us. It is a political call, not an analytical conclusion.[37] He is not turning his back on all attempts to ensure that people can live in relative safety, or even on the existence of surveillance agencies. One kind of freedom is to pursue technically supported ways of seeking human security of all kinds. But when the product of such freedom curtails the enjoyment of everyday freedoms to speak or associate with others, or to dissent from government policy, or just to live without fear, something has gone badly wrong.[38]

Surveillance will not be read in the same way after Snowden. His revelations, however incomplete, are sufficient to indicate with crystal clarity that things have to change. If they are to change in ways that enhance the common good and human flourishing – in other words, in our daily life relationships – then let us imagine a world without unnecessary secrecy, where we have opportunities to know about and approve attempts to define and improve security and in which our care for each other is expressed right down to the level of caring about what happens to personal data of all kinds.

Let us imagine a world where businesses and government departments are clear about their relationships and where opportunities exist for meaningful consultation with and intervention by independent bodies. A world where trust and care bloom and burgeon from local to global relationships, whether digital or face-to-face. Working towards such a future, politically, practically, and personally, is energized by alternative visions. And they are vital.

The coda suggests some grounded and workable ways forward.

Coda: From Words to Actions

Since Snowden, we all know much more about surveillance. This book, like several others, has put some of that into words. Chapter by chapter, we have reviewed the contexts and the meanings of surveillance today, highlighting Snowden's contribution to what we now know. Hopefully, the words will make a difference; words are powerful and can change situations.

But those situations will not change just like that, however strong or well chosen our words. What will produce transformation is practices. New practices are needed at every level, from the corporate boardroom and government committee room to what ordinary citizens and consumers do from day to day. From NSA operatives fine-tuning algorithms to high-school children going online to complete their homework, personal data have to be treated differently in a digital age. This means several things must happen.

- *Address the climate of change* We all have to start thinking more critically about the technologies we use from day to day. Using social media is not innocent fun or even a serious-but-neutral activity. As I argued earlier, changes in the everyday ways that cellphones and computers are used will contribute to much larger alterations in the ways that surveillance happens. This is a critical factor at the local level, when ordinary individuals start acting differently online.[39]
- *Share new practices* Those with some expertise, whether technical, political or educational, need to share their ideas with others. Snowden sets a stunning example here, but each of us, in our workplace and community, can help others understand what it means to use computers and cellphones in ways that do not compromise privacy, trample rights, undermine democracy. One obvious example is that those working in technical areas can argue for techniques that reduce or eliminate unnecessary surveillance. 'Privacy by design and default' is more than a mere slogan.
- *Focus on first things* What is malignantly missing in mass surveillance, as Snowden has shown, is accountability and transparency in government and commercial enterprises.

Within the welter of detailed disclosures some significant failings loom large, casting a shadow over everything. How can accountability and transparency be promoted and become part of the very structure of surveillance? This demands intervention at every level and usually through participation in organizations devoted to the task, whether professional bodies, activist groups, government committees or the like. Or through sending letters to editors, politicians and others, or writing blogs, op-eds, posts or tweets, as appropriate or possible in different circumstances.

- *Speak truth to power* The Snowden revelations touch our intimate, everyday lives in profound ways but those in highest authority need to understand this – and how to address the challenges. Opportunities must be sought to bring these matters to the urgent attention of politicians, corporate and tech leaders, judges and others with weighty influence. Different tactics are called for depending on the official in question, but well-informed approaches may be made through whatever channels are available. Numerous internet-related non-governmental organizations and lobby and pressure groups have formed disparate social movements to demand accountability for, and transparency about, the surveillance practices exposed by Snowden.[40]

- *Raise awareness of vulnerability* Snowden's work shows that everyone is susceptible to surveillance and anyone's life can unravel due to surveillance 'mistakes' and inadequacies. But some are more vulnerable than others and deserve special care and protection from the unwanted eye. Visible minorities are an obvious case in point, especially those, such as Muslims, who have been falsely fingered in the media as having terrorist tendencies. Others are also under suspicion because of the categories in which they

are classified and need equally sensitive strategies against
unwarranted suffering.

• *Leverage law and policy* Two crucial areas for action around
the world are these: One, obtaining adequate and meaningful democratic oversight of surveillance organizations,
especially intelligence agencies. This is a major, ongoing
political problem. Two, pressing for radical legal change
that acknowledges the distinctiveness of a digital era. Most
countries are living in the last century, legally speaking.
Law needs collaborative updating in both technically and
ethically sensitive ways. Each action area is vital; focusing
on one but not the other will not suffice, long term.

• *Press for change with patient persistence* This is not the
moment to relax pressure against intensifying mass surveillance, or pressure on ourselves to make practical changes.
At the same time, many of the changes that are needed do
not happen overnight. New ways of doing things often
appear at a seemingly glacial pace, especially if they are to
be embedded in our daily routines and, at the highest level,
enshrined in law. Past experiences in the US, with Water-
gate and the Church Committee, for example, took many
years to bear fruit.

• *Remember why this matters* Encryption protocols and
privacy trustmarks are important but most people do not
work with such categories. What matters is being able
to text your friend without fear, to Google without angst,
to tweet without tension, to move around the city or
meet up with fellow travellers without nervously wondering who is tracking you and why. It is participating in
public without fear, living our lives without worry about
who is watching. This is part of *human* security, involves
human relationships and is vitally linked with human
flourishing.

NOTES

Introduction: Citizenfour Alert!

Epigraph: An email, read out loud, from the opening sequence of the documentary film *Citizenfour* (2014) directed by Laura Poitras.

1 A version of this lecture has been published as D. Lyon, 'The emerging surveillance culture', in A. Jansson and M. Christiansen (eds), *Media, Surveillance and Identity* (New York: Peter Lang, 2014), pp. 71–88.

2 Previous NSA whistleblowers include Mark Klein, William Binney and Thomas Drake. Investigative journalist James Bamford and historian Matthew Aid had also thrown unwelcome light on the NSA.

3 This is a reminder, of course, that the surveillance *economy* is a vital component of the story unfolding today. See e.g. K. Ball and L. Snider (eds), *The Surveillance-Industrial Complex: Towards a Political Economy of Surveillance* (London: Routledge, 2014). This theme is also picked up in J. Assange, *When Google Met WikiLeaks* (New York: OR Books, 2014).

4 The idea of 'open source' intelligence emerged in the mid-1990s as access to online information-rich communications offered a new opportunity for intelligence gathering, but its use was not publicly obvious until after 9/11 and the growth of social media.

5 Interestingly, Snowden does not seem to comment on other relevant writers (such as Ray Bradbury, Philip K. Dick or J. G. Ballard).

6 See G. Witte, 'Snowden says government spying worse than Orwellian', *Washington Post*, 25 Dec. 2013, at http://www.washingtonpost.com/world/europe/snowden-says-spying-worse-than-orwellian/2013/12/25/e9c806aa-6d90-11e3-a5d0-6f31cd74f760_story.html.

7 See D. Altheide, 'The triumph of fear: connecting the dots about whistleblowers and surveillance', *International Journal of Cyber Warfare and Terrorism* 4.1 (2014): 1–7.

8 The story may be read in G. Greenwald, *No Place to Hide: Edward Snowden, the NSA, and the US Surveillance State* (New York: Metropolitan Books; Toronto: Signal, 2014).

9 See the Snowden Digital Surveillance Archive, project partners: Canadian Journalists for Free Expression (CJFE) and the Politics of Surveillance Project at the Faculty of Information at the University of Toronto, 2015, at https://snowdenarchive.cjfe.org/greenstone/cgi-bin/library.cgi; as well as e.g. Al Jazeera, 'Timeline of Edward Snowden revelations', Al Jazeera America, 2013, at http://america.aljazeera.com/articles/multimedia/timeline-edward-snowden-revelations.html/; and a summary for Canada at https://www.christopher-parsons.com/writings/cse-summaries/.

10 It is symptomatic of today's celebrity culture, of course, that surveillance of high-profile public figures garners much more mass media interest than the mass surveillance of ordinary – in this case German – citizens. At the same time, it is not only the NSA that spies on others' leaders: Germany has also kept tabs on prominent Americans such as John Kerry and Hillary Clinton. See M. Williams, 'Germany "spied" on John Kerry and Hillary Clinton – Der Spiegel', *The Guardian*, 16 Aug. 2014, at

http://www.theguardian.com/world/2014/aug/16/germany -spied-john-kerry-hillary-clinton-der-spiegel/.

11 See D. Rushe, 'Sim card database hack gave US and UK access to billions of cellphones', *The Guardian*, 19 Feb. 2015, at http:// www.theguardian.com/us-news/2015/feb/19/nsa-gchq-sim -card-billions-cellphones-hacking.

12 See G. Weston, G. Greenwald and R. Gallagher, 'New Snowden docs show US spied during G20 in Toronto', *CBC News*, 27 Nov. 2013, at http://www.cbc.ca/m/touch/news/ story/1.2442448/.

13 See L. Kelion, 'Snowden leaks: GCHQ "spied on Facebook and YouTube"', *BBC News*, 28 Jan. 2014, at http://www.bbc.com/ news/technology-25927844.

14 See C. Bennett, K. Haggerty, D. Lyon and V. Steeves (eds), *Transparent Lives: Surveillance in Canada* (also *Vivre à nu. La surveillance au Canada*) (Edmonton: Athabasca University Press, 2014), at http://www.aupress.ca/index.php/books/120237.

15 See N. M. Richards and J. H. King, 'Three paradoxes of big data', *Stanford Law Review Online* 66.41 (2013): 41–6.

16 'Connecting the dots' is a term associated with the US Department of Homeland Security. It likens the quest for usable information to a children's puzzle in which a picture appears when dots on the page are connected with a pencil line. The *9/11 Commission Report* continued to justify use of the term, saying that 'the importance of integrated, all-source analysis cannot be overstated. Without it, it is not possible to "connect the dots".' See 9-11 Commission, *The 9/11 Commission Report*, National Commission on Terrorist Attacks upon the United States, 2004, at http://govinfo.library.unt.edu/911/ report/.

17 A reference to Spielberg's 2002 sci-fi thriller set in the US in 2054 when a Pre-crime Department uses special means to prevent crime, especially murder, from occurring – before it happens.

18 See Z. Bauman and D. Lyon, *Liquid Surveillance: A Conversation* (Cambridge: Polity, 2013).

19 See Ball and Snider, *The Surveillance-Industrial Complex*.

Chapter 1   Snowden Storm

Epigraph: Interview with Alan Rusbridger and Ewen MacAskill, see 'Edward Snowden interview – the edited transcript', *The Guardian*, 18 July 2014, at http://www.theguardian.com/ world/2014/jul/18/-sp-edward-snowden-nsa-whistleblower -interview-transcript/.

1 Questions of democracy, accountability and the politics of surveillance are examined more fully in chapters 4 and 5.

2 See M. Klein, *Wiring up the Big Brother Machine... and Fighting It* (Charleston, SC: Booksurge, 2009); J. Bamford, *The Shadow Factory: The Ultra-Secret NSA from 9/11 to the Eavesdropping on America* (New York: Doubleday, 2008).

3 See A. Clement, 'NSA surveillance: exploring the geographies of internet interception', in *iConference 2014 Proceedings* (2014), pp. 412–25, doi:10.9776/14119, at https://www.ideals.illinois. edu/bitstream/handle/2142/47305/119_ready.pdf?sequence=2.

4 See G. Greenwald 'The NSA's mass and indiscriminate spying on Brazilians', *The Guardian*, 7 July 2013, at http://www. theguardian.com/commentisfree/2013/jul/07/nsa-brazilians -globo-spying/.

5 See B. Gellman and T. Lindeman, 'Inner workings of a top-secret spy program', *Washington Post*, 29 June 2013, at http:// apps.washingtonpost.com/g/page/national/inner-workings -of-a-top-secret-spy-program/282/.

6 See Spiegel staff, 'Quantum spying: GCHQ used fake LinkedIn pages to target engineers', *Der Spiegel*, 11 Nov. 2013, at http:// www.spiegel.de/international/world/ghcq-targets-engineers -with-fake-linkedin-pages-a-932821.html.

7 See D. Murakami Wood and K. Ball, 'Brandscapes of control? Surveillance, marketing and the co-construction of subjectivity and space in neo-liberal capitalism', *Marketing Theory* 13.1 (2013): 47–67.

8 See J. Mayer, 'The secret sharer', *New Yorker*, 23 May 2011, at http://www.newyorker.com/magazine/2011/05/23/the-secret -sharer/.

9 Weber and Arendt have much to say about what is now known as surveillance, in relation to maintaining bureaucratic records on individuals (Weber) or how power is generated in 'spaces of appearance' (Arendt). See e.g. C. Dandeker, *Surveillance, Power and Modernity* (Cambridge: Polity, 1990) and X. Marquez, 'Spaces of appearance and spaces of surveillance', *Polity* 44 (2012): 6–31.

10 See the argument in D. Lyon, *The Electronic Eye: The Rise of the Surveillance Society* (Cambridge: Polity, 1994), ch. 2.

11 See G. Greenwald, 'NSA collecting phone records of millions of Verizon customers daily', *The Guardian*, 5 June 2013, at http://www.theguardian.com/world/2013/jun/06/nsa-phone -records-verizon-court-order/.

12 See D. Lyon (ed.), *Surveillance as Social Sorting: Privacy, Risk and Digital Discrimination* (London: Routledge, 2003).

13 See P. Regan, *Legislating Privacy: Technology, Social Values and Public Policy* (1995; Durham: University of North Carolina Press, 2009); C. Bennett and C. Raab, *The Governance of Privacy: Policy Instruments in Global Perspective* (Cambridge, MA: MIT Press, 2006); and V. Steeves, 'Reclaiming the social value of privacy', in I. Kerr, C. Lucock and V. Steeves (eds), *Lessons from the Identity Trail: Anonymity, Privacy and Identity in a Networked Age* (Oxford: Oxford University Press, 2009).

14 See e.g. F. J. Smist, Jr, *Congress Oversees the United States Intelligence Community, 1947–1989* (Knoxville: University of Tennessee Press, 1990), and final report of the Royal Commission of Inquiry into Certain Activities of the Royal Canadian Mounted Police (McDonald Commission), Ottawa, 1981.

15 For a no-holds-barred critique see H. Giroux, 'Totalitarian paranoia in the post-Orwellian surveillance state', *Cultural Studies*, online 14 May 2014, at http://dx.doi.org/10.1080/0950 2386.2014.917118.

16 See e.g. 'We know where you live', *NOVA*, PBS documentary, season 17, aired 27 Nov. 1990, and later the book by E. Larsen, *The Naked Consumer: How Our Private Lives Become Public Commodities* (New York: Penguin Books, 1994).

17 See G. Marx, *Undercover: Police Surveillance in America* (Berkeley: University of California Press, 1988), p. 207.

18 These developments are discussed in Lyon, *The Electronic Eye*, D. Lyon, *Surveillance Society: Monitoring Everyday Life* (Buckingham, UK: Open University Press, 2001) and D. Lyon, *Surveillance Studies: An Overview* (Cambridge: Polity, 2007).

19 See Lyon, *Surveillance Society*, and D. Murakami Wood (ed.), *A Report on the Surveillance Society* (Wilmslow, UK: Office of the Information Commissioner, 2006) and the summary report at https://ico.org.uk/media/about-the-ico/documents/1042391/surveillance-society-summary-06.pdf.

20 See D. Lyon, *Surveillance after September 11* (Cambridge: Polity, 2003), pp. 92f. An excellent treatment of the TIA program is S. Harris, *The Watchers* (London: Penguin, 2013).

21 See A. Marwick, 'The public domain: social surveillance in everyday life', *Surveillance & Society* 9.4 (2012): 378–93, at http://library.queensu.ca/ojs/index.php/surveillance-and-soc iety/article/viewFile/pub_dom/pub_dom/; D. Trottier, *Social Media as Surveillance* (London: Ashgate, 2012).

22 See J. Lynch, 'New FOIA documents reveal DHS social media monitoring during Obama inauguration', Electronic Frontier Foundation, 13 Oct. 2010, at https://www.eff.org/deeplinks/2010/10/new-foia-documents-reveal-dhs-social-media/.

23 See K. S. Ball and F. Webster (eds), *The Intensification of Surveillance* (London: Pluto Press, 2003).

24 See D. Lyon, 'Surveillance, Snowden and big data: capacities, consequences, critique', *Big Data & Society* 1.1 (2014), at http://bds.sagepub.com/content/1/2/2053951714541861.abstract/.

25 Formerly on the Defense Advanced Research Projects Agency (DARPA) website at www.darpa.mil/iao/TIAsystems.htm/.

26 See e.g. G. Keizer, *Privacy* (New York: Picador, 2012).

27 See Lyon, 'Surveillance, Snowden and big data'.

28 For more on this, see C. Bennett, K. Haggerty, D. Lyon and V. Steeves (eds), *Transparent Lives: Surveillance in Canada* (also *Vivre à nu. La surveillance au Canada*) (Edmonton: Athabasca University Press, 2014), at http://www.aupress.ca/index.php/books/120237.

29 See E. Taylor, *Surveillance Schools: Security, Discipline and Control in Contemporary Education* (London: Macmillan, 2013).

30 See G. Agamben, 'For a theory of destituent power', *Chronos*, public lecture in Athens, 16 Nov. 2013, at http://www.chronosmag.eu/index.php/g-agamben-for-a-theory-of-destituent-power.html.

31 See e.g. D. Lyon and Ö. Topak, 'Promoting global identification: corporations, IGOs and ID card systems', in K. Ball and L. Snider (eds), *The Surveillance-Industrial Complex: Towards a Political Economy of Surveillance* (London: Routledge, 2014), pp. 27–43.

32 See V. Mosco, *To the Cloud: Big Data in a Turbulent World* (Boulder, CO: Paradigm, 2014), p. 77.

33 Mosco, *To the Cloud*.

34 See M. Marquis-Boire, 'Schrodinger's cat video and the death of clear-text', Citizen Lab, Research Brief 46, 15 Aug. 2014, at https://citizenlab.org/2014/08/cat-video-and-the-death-of-clear-text/.

35 See C. Timberg and E. Nakashima, 'Agreements with private companies protect access to cables' data for surveillance', *Washington Post*, 6 July 2013, at http://www.washingtonpost.com/business/technology/agreements-with-private-companies-protect-us-access-to-cables-data-for-surveillance/2013/07/06/aa5d017a-df77-11e2-b2d4-ea6d8f477a01_story.html.

36 See map in Bennett et al., *Transparent Lives*, p. 113.

37 Such as Dropbox; see Z. Bauman, D. Bigo, P. Esteves, E. Guild, V. Jabri, D. Lyon and R. B. Walker, 'After Snowden: rethinking the impact of surveillance', *International Political Sociology* 8.2 (2014): 121–44, at 123.

38 See R. Gallagher and G. Greenwald, 'Canada casts global surveillance dragnet over file downloads', *The Intercept*, 28 Jan. 2015, at https://firstlook.org/theintercept/2015/01/28/canada-cse-levitation-mass-surveillance.

39 See e.g. D. Bigo, 'Globalized (in)security: the field and the banopticon', in D. Bigo and A. Tsouskala (eds), *Terror, Insecurity and Liberty* (London: Routledge, 2008). See also Bauman et al., 'After Snowden', 124–31, and Lyon and Topak, 'Promoting global identification'.

40 See Bauman et al., 'After Snowden', 125.

41 See Ball and Snider, *The Surveillance-Industrial Complex*.

42 See K. Haggerty and R. Ericson, *Policing the Risk Society* (Toronto: University of Toronto Press, 1997).
43 See J. P. Brodeur, *The Policing Web* (Oxford: Oxford University Press, 2010).
44 Particularly with the help of units such as the Oxford Internet Institute in the UK, at http://www.oii.ox.ac.uk, or the Pew 'Internet and American Life' project in the US, at http://www.pewinternet.org.
45 See e.g. C. Fuchs, *Social Media: A Critical Introduction* (London: Sage, 2014); Marwick, 'The public domain'; Trottier, *Social Media as Surveillance*.
46 See Giroux, 'Totalitarian paranoia'.
47 See the research papers of Social Networking Sites in the Surveillance Society, at www.sns3.uti.at.dd29412.kasserver.com/?page_id=24.
48 Bennett et al., *Transparent Lives*, p. 84.

Chapter 2 World Watching

Epigraph: 'Edward Snowden SXSW: full transcript and video', SXSW conference, Austin, Texas, *Inside blog*, 10 Mar. 2014, at http://blog.inside.com/blog/2014/3/10/edward-snowden-sxsw-full-transcription-and-video.
1 See D. E. Sanger and M. Fackler, 'NSA breached North Korean networks before Sony attack, officials say', *New York Times*, 18 Jan. 2015, at http://www.nytimes.com/2015/01/19/world/asia/nsa-tapped-into-north-korean-networks-before-sony-attack-officials-say.html.
2 See J. Appelbaum, A. Gibson, C. Guarnieri, A. Muller-Maguhn, L. Poitras, M. Rosenbach, L. Ryge, H. Schmundt and M. Sontheimer, 'The digital arms race: NSA preps America for future battle', *Der Spiegel*, 17 Jan. 2015, at http://www.spiegel.de/international/world/new-snowden-docs-indicate-scope-of-nsa-preparations-for-cyber-battle-a-1013409.html.
3 See J. Kirk, 'Google to encrypt Cloud Storage data by default', *PC World*, 15 Aug. 2013, at http://www.pcworld.com/article/2046802/google-to-encrypt-cloud-storage-data-by-default.html.

4 See G. Greenwald, *No Place to Hide: Edward Snowden, the NSA and the US Surveillance State* (New York: Metropolitan Books, 2014), p. 6.

5 See D. Lyon, 'A sociology of information', in C. Calhoun, C. Rojek and B. Turner (eds), *The Sage Handbook of Sociology* (London: Sage, 2005).

6 The career of John Poindexter is worth a comment. Before his involvement in TIA he was a US naval officer and then a NSA adviser in the Reagan years. He was convicted for felony, on several charges, relating to his role in the Iran-Contra affair, in 1990 but the conviction was overturned in 1991.

7 See I. de Sola Pool, *Technologies of Freedom* (Cambridge, MA: Harvard University Press, 1983).

8 'Data packets' are units of formatted data that are switched through networks clustered together rather than in a 'bitstream'. Different networks support the different types of traffic.

9 One of my first books on this theme was D. Lyon, *The Information Society: Issues and Illusions* (Cambridge: Polity, 1988).

10 See M. Hand, *Making Digital Cultures* (London: Ashgate, 2008).

11 This is discussed as a key surveillance trend in C. Bennett, K. Haggerty, D. Lyon and V. Steeves, *Transparent Lives: Surveillance in Canada* (Edmonton: Athabasca University Press, 2014).

12 This story is well told in R. Kitchin, *The Data Revolution* (London: Sage, 2014), ch. 5.

13 This is discussed in D. Lyon, *Surveillance after September 11* (Cambridge: Polity, 2003).

14 The Freedom of Information (FoI) requests were made by the Electronic Privacy Information Center; see 'EPIC v. Department of Homeland Security: media monitoring', Electronic Information Privacy Information Center, at https://epic.org/foia/epic-v-dhs-media-monitoring/.

15 'Cyberspace' appeared first in W. Gibson, 'Burning Chrome', *Omni*, July 1982, and more fully in W. Gibson, *Neuromancer* (New York: Ace, 1984).

16 See P. Edwards, *Closed Worlds: Computers and the Politics of Discourse in Cold War America* (Cambridge, MA: MIT Press, 1996).

17 See N. Wiener, 'The machine as threat and promise' (1953), in N. Wiener, *Collected Works and Commentaries*, ed. P. Masani (Cambridge, MA: MIT Press, 1985), vol. 4, pp. 673–8.

18 Examples include Marshall McLuhan and his teacher Harold Adams Innis.

19 See S. Gerovitch, 'The cybernetics scare and the origins of the internet', *Baltic Worlds* 11.1 (2010): 32–8, at http://balticworlds. com/the-cybernetics-scare-and-the-origins-of-the-internet/.

20 This was a strong feature of the work of Jacques Ellul – see e.g. *The Technological Society* (New York: Vintage, 1967) – in the 1960s and continues in other ways in e.g. V. Mosco, *The Digital Sublime* (Cambridge, MA: MIT Press, 2004).

21 See B. Gellman and A. Soltani, 'NSA infiltrates links to Yahoo, Google data centers worldwide, Snowden documents say', *Washington Post*, 30 Oct. 2013, at http://www.washingtonpost. com/world/national-security/nsa-infiltrates-links-to-yahoo -google-data-centers-worldwide-snowden-documents -say/2013/10/30/e51d661e-4166-11e3-8b74-d89d714ca4dd _story.html/.

22 See L. Austin, 'Lawful illegality: what Snowden has taught us about the legal infrastructure of the surveillance state', in M. Geist (ed.), *Law, Privacy and Surveillance in Canada in a Post-Snowden Era* (Ottawa: University of Ottawa Press, 2015).

23 For a theological inflection of this point see D. Lyon, 'Being post-secular in the social sciences: Taylor's social imaginaries', *New Blackfriars* 91 (2010): 648–62, esp. 51–2.

24 See Lyon, 'A sociology of information'.

25 See M. Castells, *The Information Age: Economy, Society and Culture*, vol. 1: *The Rise of the Network Society* (Oxford: Blackwell, 1996; 2nd edn 2000), vol. 2: *The Power of Identity* (Oxford: Blackwell, 1997; 2nd edn 2004), vol. 3: *End of Millennium* (Oxford: Blackwell, 1998; 2nd edn 2000).

26 See M. Castells, *The Internet Galaxy* (Oxford: Oxford University Press, 2001), p. 170. See the discussion in D. Trottier and D. Lyon, 'Key features of social media surveillance', in C. Fuchs, K. Boersma, A. Albrechtslund and M. Sandova (eds), *Internet and Surveillance: Challenges of Web 2.0 and Social Media* (London: Routledge, 2012).

27 See M. Castells, *Communication Power* (Oxford: Oxford University Press, 2009), p. 55, cited in C. Fuchs, 'Critique of the political economy of Web 2.0 surveillance', in Fuchs et al., *Internet and Surveillance*.

28 This kind of analysis of information power originates in the work of H. A. Innis, *The Bias of Communication* (Toronto: University of Toronto Press, 1962).

29 See H. Menzies, 'Digital networks: the medium of communication, and the message', *Canadian Journal of Communication* 24.4 (1999), at http://www.cjc-online.ca/index.php/journal/article/view/1125/1033/.

30 See G. Coleman, *Hacker, Hoaxer, Whistleblower, Spy: The Many Faces of Anonymous* (London: Verso, 2014).

31 See S. Bok, *Secrets: The Ethics of Concealment and Revelation* (New York: Vintage, 1989).

32 G. Greenwald, 'Cash, weapons and surveillance: the US is a key party to every Israeli attack', *The Intercept*, 4 Aug. 2014, at https://firstlook.org/theintercept/2014/08/04/cash-weapons-surveillance/.

33 See A. Clement, 'Canada's bad dream', *World Policy Journal* (Fall 2014), at http://www.worldpolicy.org/journal/fall2014/canada%27s-bad-dream/.

34 See G. Weston, G. Greenwald and R. Gallagher, 'New Snowden docs show U.S. spied during G20 in Toronto', *CBC News*, 1 Dec. 2013, at http://www.cbc.ca/news/politics/new-snowden-docs-show-u-s-spied-during-g20-in-toronto-1.2442448/.

35 See Clement, 'Canada's bad dream'.

36 More detailed analysis is available in Clement, 'Canada's bad dream'.

37 See e.g. R. Clarke, M. Morell, G. Stone, C. Sunstein and P. Swire, *The NSA Report: Liberty and Security in a Changing World* (Princeton: Princeton University Press, 2014).

38 See E. MacAskill, 'Independent commission to investigate future of internet after NSA revelations', *The Guardian*, 22 Jan. 2014, at http://www.theguardian.com/world/2014/jan/22/independent-commission-future-internet-nsa-revelations-davos/.

39 See L. Harding, 'Mass surveillance is fundamental threat to human rights, says European report', *The Guardian*,

26 Jan. 2015, at http://www.theguardian.com/world/2015/
jan/26/mass-surveillance-threat-human-rights-council-europe.
40 See e.g. C. J. Bennett, *The Privacy Advocates: Resisting the Spread
of Surveillance* (Cambridge MA: MIT Press, 2008).
41 See Clarke et al., *The NSA Report*, pp. 24, 35.
42 See C. Savage and L. Poitras, 'How a court secretly evolved,
extending US spies' reach', *New York Times*, 11 Mar. 2014, at
http://www.nytimes.com/2014/03/12/us/how-a-courts-secret
-evolution-extended-spies-reach.html?_r=0.
43 See E. Donahoe and M. L. Canineu, 'A year after Snowden, a
watershed moment for internet freedom', *Globe and Mail*, 18
June 2014, at http://www.theglobeandmail.com/globe-debate/
a-year-after-snowden-weve-reached-a-watershed-moment-for
-web-freedom/article19215294/).
44 See T. Falchetta, 'Building the foundations: surveillance
and the right to privacy at the UN in 2014', *Privacy International*, 18 Dec. 2014, at https://www.privacyinternational.
org/?q=node/93.
45 See R. Deibert, *Black Code: Surveillance, Privacy and the Dark
Side of the Internet* (Toronto: Signal, 2013).
46 On this, see A. Dworkin, 'Surveillance, privacy and security:
Europe's confused response to Snowden', European Council of
Foreign Relations, 20 Jan. 2015, at http://www.ecfr.eu/publica
tions/summary/mass_surveillance_privacy_and_security
_europes_confused_response329/.

Chapter 3 Menacing Metadata

Epigraph: Edward Snowden by video link to Moment of Truth
event, quoted by Stilgherrian, 'Can Snowden finally kill the
"harmless metadata" myth?', *ZDNet*, 16 September 2014, at
http://www.zdnet.com/article/can-snowden-finally-kill-the
-harmless-metadata-myth/.
1 Matt Blaze, University of Pennsylvania, quoted in J. Naughton,
'NSA surveillance: don't underestimate the extraordinary power

of metadata', *The Guardian*, 21 June 2013, at http://www.the
guardian.com/technology/2013/jun/21/nsa-surveillance-meta
data-content-obama. The *Zeit Online* article, 'Tell-all telephone', with interactive display is at www.zeit.de/datenschutz/
malte-spitz-data-retention.

2 See S. Ackerman, 'Roy Wyden: NSA review panel offers "substantial, meaningful reforms"', *The Guardian*, 19 Dec. 2013, at
http://www.theguardian.com/world/2013/dec/18/nsa-review
-panel-reform-ron-wyden/.

3 See P. Moskowitz, 'Report suggests NSA surveillance has not
stopped terrorism', Al Jazeera America, 13 Jan. 2014, at http://
america.aljazeera.com/articles/2014/1/13/review-finds
-nsametadatacollectionhasntstoppedanattack.html/.

4 See S. Harris, 'Metadata may not catch many terrorists but it's
great at busting journalists' sources', *Foreign Policy*, 24 Sept.
2013, at http://blog.foreignpolicy.com/posts/2013/09/24/meta
data_may_not_catch_many_terrorists_but_its_great_at
_busting_journalists_sources/.

5 Online video, with G. Greenwald, E. MacAskill and L. Poitras,
'Edward Snowden: the whistleblower behind the NSA surveillance revelations', *The Guardian*, 11 June 2013, at http://www.
theguardian.com/world/2013/jun/09/edward-snowden-nsa
-whistleblower-surveillance.

6 See d. boyd and K. Crawford, 'Critical questions for big data:
provocations for a cultural, technological, and scholarly phenomenon', *Information, Communication & Society* 15.5 (2012):
662–79.

7 See C. Bennett, K. Haggerty, D. Lyon and V. Steeves (eds),
Transparent Lives: Surveillance in Canada (also *Vivre à nu. La
surveillance au Canada*) (Edmonton: Athabasca University Press,
2014), at http://www.aupress.ca/index.php/books/120237.

8 See K. Haggerty and R. Ericson, 'The surveillant assemblage',
British Journal of Sociology 51.4 (2000): 605–22.

9 See O. H. Gandy, Jr, *Coming to Terms with Chance: Engaging
Rational Discrimination and Cumulative Disadvantage* (Burling-
ton, VA: Ashgate, 2012), p. 125.

10 See e.g. M. Andrejevic and K. Gates, 'Big data surveillance: introduction', *Surveillance & Society* 12.2 (2014): 185–96.
11 Cited in D. Storm, 'Snowden warns that UK's Tempora "snarfs" everything, even worse than NSA's PRISM', *Computerworld*, 8 July 2013, at http://www.computerworld.com/article/2473959/data-privacy/snowden-warns-tempora-surveillance-snarfs –everything–even–worse–than–nsa–s–prism.html/.
12 See J. Lanchester, 'The Snowden files: why the British public should be worried about GCHQ', *The Guardian*, 3 Oct. 2013, at http://www.theguardian.com/world/2013/oct/03/edward-sn owden-files-john-lanchester.
13 See A. Rutkin, 'Just four credit card clues can identify anyone', *New Scientist*, 29 Jan. 2015, at http://www.newscientist.com/article/dn26879-just-four-credit-card-clues-can-identify-any one.html#.VM_dJsboV7m.
14 See R. Kitchin, 'Thinking critically about and researching algorithms', Social Science Research Network, 28 Oct. 2014, at http://papers.ssrn.com/sol3/papers.cfm?abstract_id=2515786, and F. Kraemer, K. van Overveld and M. Peterson, 'Is there an ethics of algorithms?', *Ethics of Information Technology* 13 (2011): 251–60.
15 See 'Intelligence budget data', FAS (Federation of American Scientists), at http://www.fas.org/irp/budget/index.html?PHPS ESSID1/470809 e6b347db7b2122df1ef24d743e0/.
16 See B. C. Newell, 'The massive metadata machine: liberty, power and secret mass surveillance in the U.S. and Europe', *I/S: A Journal of Law and Policy for the Information Society* 10.2 (2014): 481–522.
17 See L. Payton, 'Spy agencies, prime minister's adviser defend Wi-Fi data collection', *CBC News*, 3 Feb. 2014, at http://www. cbc.ca/news/politics/spy-agencies-prime-minister-s-adviser -defend-wi-fi-data-collection-1.2521166.
18 See C. Freeze, 'Canada's metadata collection worries critics', *Globe and Mail*, 27 Mar. 2014, at http://www.theglobeandmail. com/news/politics/canadas-metadata-collection-worries-crit ics/article17714407/.

19 See B. Schneier, 'CSEC analysis of IP and user data', 2014, at https://www.schneier.com/blog/archives/2014/02/csec_surveillan.html.

20 B. Gellman and A. Soltani, 'NSA infiltrates links to Yahoo, Google data centers worldwide, Snowden documents say', *Washington Post*, 30 Oct. 2013, at http://www.washingtonpost. com/world/national-security/nsa-infiltrates-links-to-yahoo -google-data-centers-worldwide-snowden-documents -say/2013/10/30/e51d661e-4166-11e3-8b74-d89d714ca4dd _story.html.

21 See J. Podesta, 'Big data and the future of privacy', 23 Jan. 2014, at https://www.whitehouse.gov/blog/2014/01/23/big-data-and -future-privacy.

22 See M. Savage, 'Digital fields, networks and capital: sociology beyond structures and fluids', in K. Orton-Johnson and N. Prior (eds), *Digital Sociology: Critical Perspectives* (Basingstoke, UK: Palgrave Macmillan, 2013), pp. 139–50.

23 See J. van Dijck, 'Datafication, dataism and dataveillance: Big Data between scientific paradigm and ideology', *Surveillance & Society* 12.2 (2014), at http://library.queensu.ca/ojs/index.php/ surveillance-and-society/article/view/datafication.

24 See R. Clarke, 'Information technology and dataveillance', *Communications of the ACM* 31.5 (1988): 498–512, and 'Data-veillance – 15 years on', 2003, at http://www.rogerclarke.com/ DV/DVNZ03.html#DT.

25 See J. Bertolucci, 'Big data's new buzzword: datafication', *Information Week*, 25 Feb. 2013, at http://www.informationweek. com/big-data/big-data-analytics/big-datas-new-buzzword -datafication/d/d-id/1108797.

26 See K. S. Bankston and A. Soltani, 'Tiny constables and the cost of surveillance: making cents out of *United States v. Jones*', *Yale Law Journal* 123 (9 Jan. 2014), at http://www.yalelawjournal. org/forum/tiny-constables-and-the-cost-of-surveillance -making-cents-out-of-united-states-v-jones.

27 See I. Kerr and J. Earle, 'Prediction, preemption, presumption: how big data threatens big picture privacy', *Stanford Law Review*

Online 66 (3 Sept. 2013), at http://www.stanfordlawreview.org/online/privacy-and-big-data/prediction-preemption-presumption.

28 See R. Kitchin, 'The real-time city? Big data and smart urbanism', *GeoJournal* 79 (2014): 1–14, and R. Kitchin, *The Data Revolution: Big Data, Open Data, Data Infrastructures and Their Consequences* (London: Sage, 2014).

29 See D. Trottier, *Social Media as Surveillance: Rethinking Visibility in a Converging World* (London: Ashgate, 2012).

30 See L. A. Amoore, 'Data derivatives: on the emergence of a security risk calculus for our times', *Theory, Culture & Society* 28 (2011): 24–43.

31 See M. Savage and R. Burrows, 'The coming crisis of empirical sociology', *Sociology* 44.5 (2007): 885–99.

32 See M. J. Glennon, 'National security and double government', *Harvard National Security Journal* 5.1 (2014): 1–113.

33 See E. Ruppert, 'The governmental topologies of database devices', *Theory, Culture & Society* 29.4–5 (2012): 116–36, at 118.

34 See e.g. D. Lyon, *Surveillance Society: Monitoring Everyday Life* (Buckingham, UK: Open University Press, 2001).

35 See e.g. E. Larsen, *The Naked Consumer* (New York: Penguin, 1994).

36 See N. Green and S. Smith, 'A spy in your pocket', *Surveillance & Society* 1.4 (2004): 573–87.

37 See A. Mattelart and A. Vitalis, *Le profilage des populations. Du livret ouvrier au cybercontrôle* (Paris: La Découverte, 2014).

38 See D. Bigo, 'Diagonal mass surveillance: Gulliver against the Lilliputians', OpenDemocracy, 5 Mar. 2014, at https://www.opendemocracy.net/can-europe-make-it/didier-bigo/diagonal-mass-surveillance-gulliver-versus-lilliputians/.

39 See D. Citron, 'Technological due process', *Washington University Law Review* 85.6 (2008): 1249–313, at http://openscholarship.wustl.edu/cgi/viewcontent.cgi?article=1166&context=law_lawreview.

40 Citron, 'Technological due process'. As new 'lawful access' powers are developed (e.g. in Canada in 2015), the lack of public

reporting and individual notification, and the gag orders placed on those responsible for effecting the changes are likely to become causes for alarm among privacy lawyers and scholars.

41 See G. Genosko, 'Tense theory: the temporalities of surveillance', in D. Lyon (ed.), *Theorizing Surveillance* (Cullompton, UK: Willan, 2006).

42 See U. Franklin, *The Real World of Technology* (Toronto: Anansi, 1990), p. 41.

43 See Kerr and Earle, 'Prediction, preemption, presumption'.

44 See A. Regalado, 'The data made me do it', *Technology Review*, 3 May 2013, at http://www.technologyreview.com/news/514346/the-data-made-me-do-it/.

45 See D. Butler, 'When Google got flu wrong', *Nature* 494.7436 (2013): 155–6, at http://www.nature.com/news/when-google-got-flu-wrong-1.12413/.

46 See M. De Goede, 'The politics of privacy in the age of preemptive security', *International Political Sociology* 8.1 (2014): 101–4.

47 See L. Amoore, 'Security and the incalculable', *Security Dialogue* 45.5 (2014): 423–39.

48 Amoore, 'Security and the incalculable'.

49 See S. Gallagher, 'What the NSA can do with "big data"', Ars Electronica, 11 June 2013, at http://arstechnica.com/information-technology/2013/06/what-the-nsa-can-do-with-big-data/.

50 See https://nsa.gov1.info/utah-data-center/.

51 The early debate may be read in T. B. Lee, 'Here's everything we know about PRISM to date', *Washington Post*, 12 June 2013, at http://www.washingtonpost.com/blogs/wonkblog/wp/2013/06/12/heres-everything-we-know-about-prism-to-date/.

52 See e.g. J. Turow, *The Daily You: How the New Advertising Industry Is Defining Your Identity and Your Worth* (New Haven: Yale University Press, 2012); O. Gandy, *Coming to Terms with Chance: Engaging Rational Discrimination and Cumulative Disadvantage* (London: Ashgate. 2013).

53 See L. Gitelman (ed.), *"Raw Data" Is an Oxymoron* (Cambridge, MA: MIT Press, 2013).

54 See G. Bowker, 'Data flakes', in Gitelman, *"Raw Data" Is an Oxymoron*.

Chapter 4 Precarious Privacy

Epigraph: Edward Snowden, 'Here's how we take back the Internet', TED Talks, March 2014, at http://www.ted.com/talks/edward_snowden_here_s_how_we_take_back_the_internet/.

1 See G. Greenwald and M. Hussain, 'Under surveillance: meet the Muslim-American leaders the FBI and NSA have been spying on', *The Intercept*, 7 Sept. 2014, at https://firstlook.org/theintercept/article/2014/07/09/under-surveillance/.

2 See S. Ackerman, 'FBI teaches agents: "mainstream" Muslims are "violent, radical"', *Wired*, 14 Sept. 2011, at http://www.wired.com/2011/09/fbi-muslims-radical/.

3 See D. Rushe, 'Edward Snowden calls for greater online privacy in Reset the Net campaign', *The Guardian*, 5 June 2014, and Edward Snowden's address via satellite to Personal Democracy Forum conference, New York.

4 See E. Zureik, 'The cross-cultural study of privacy', in E. Zureik, L. L. Harling Stalker, E. Smith, D. Lyon and Y. E. Chan (eds), *Surveillance, Privacy and the Globalization of Personal Information* (Montreal and Kingston: McGill-Queen's University Press, 2010), p. 10.

5 See 'The right to privacy in the digital age', at http://www.ohchr.org/EN/Issues/DigitalAge/Pages/DigitalAgeIndex.aspx.

6 See D. Lyon, *Surveillance after September 11* (Cambridge: Polity, 2003).

7 Jacques Ellul, for instance, commented on this in the 1960s but, by and large, warnings like his were left unheeded, see J. Ellul, *The Technological Society* (New York: Vintage, 1967).

8 See D. Campbell and S. Connor, *On the Record: Surveillance, Computers and Privacy* (London: Michael Joseph, 1986); and G. T. Marx, *Undercover: Police Surveillance in America* (Berkeley: University of California Press, 1988).

9   See K. Haggerty and R. Ericson, *Policing the Risk Society* (Toronto: University of Toronto Press, 1997).

10 See D. E. Sanger and M. Apuzzo, 'Officials defend N.S.A. after new privacy details are reported', *New York Times*, 6 July 2014, at http://www.nytimes.com/2014/07/07/us/officials-defend-nsa -after-new-privacy-details-are-reported.html?emc=edit_th_201 40707&nl=todaysheadlines&nlid=55961761&_r=0/

11 See G. Greenwald, *No Place to Hide: Edward Snowden, the NSA, and the US Surveillance State* (New York: Metropolitan Books and Toronto: Signal, 2014), pp. 171–2.

12 See B. Gellman and A. Soltani, 'NSA surveillance program reaches "into the past" to retrieve, replay phone calls', *Washington Post*, 18 Mar. 2014, at http://www.washingtonpost.com/ world/national-security/nsa-surveillance-program-reaches-into -the-past-to-retrieve-replay-phone-calls/2014/03/18/ 226d2646-ade9-11e3-a49e-76adc9210f19_story.html.

13 See Spiegel staff, 'Inside TAO: documents reveal top NSA hacking unit', *Spiegel Online*, 29 Dec. 2013, at http://www. spiegel.de/international/world/the-nsa-uses-powerful-toolbox -in-effort-to-spy-on-global-networks-a-940969.html.

14 See CIGI-Ipsos, 'CIGI-Ipsos global survey on internet security and trust', Center for International Governance Innovation (CIGI) and Ipsos, 2014, at https://www.cigionline.org/internet -survey.

15 The fuller debate is rehearsed, helpfully, in C. Bennett, 'In defence of privacy: the concept and the regime', *Surveillance & Society* 8.4 (2011): 485–96, at http://library.queensu.ca/ojs/ index.php/surveillance-and-society/article/view/4184/4186/.

16 See H. Nissenbaum, *Privacy in Context: Technology, Policy and the Integrity of Social Life* (Stanford: Stanford Law Books, 2009).

17 See V. Steeves, *Young Canadians in a Wired World, Phase III: Online Privacy, Online Publicity*. Ottawa: MediaSmarts, 2014, at http://mediasmarts.ca/sites/mediasmarts/files/pdfs/publica- tion-report/full/YCWWIII_Online_Privacy_Online_Publicity _FullReport.pdf/.

18 See J. Cohen, *Configuring the Networked Self: Law, Code, and the Play of Everyday Practice* (New Haven: Yale University Press, 2012).

19 See Bennett 'In defence of privacy', p. 5.

20 The idea of the 'relational' as basic to human being is found in several philosophical and religious traditions. It is at the heart of the Christian tradition, for example, especially in teaching on the Trinity, where God is seen as indivisibly social. If human beings are the *imago dei* – the 'image of God' – then here is a shared characteristic par excellence.

21 See C. Fieschi, 'The social value of privacy', in C. Edwards and C. Fieschi (eds), *UK Confidential* (London: Demos, 2008), at http://www.demos.co.uk/files/UK%20confidential%20-%20 web.pdf.

22 This is discussed by Z. Bauman and D. Lyon, *Liquid Surveillance* (Cambridge: Polity, 2013), pp. 26–34.

23 See e.g. Cohen, *Configuring the Networked Self*.

24 See V. Steeves, 'Reclaiming the social value of privacy', in I. Kerr, C. Lucock and V. Steeves (eds), *Lessons from the Identity Trail: Anonymity, Privacy and Identity in a Networked Age* (Oxford: Oxford University Press, 2009).

25 I think especially of Bennett, 'In defence of privacy'.

26 J. Ball, 'GCHQ captured emails of journalists from top international media', *The Guardian*, 19 Jan. 2015, at http://www.theguardian.com/uk-news/2015/jan/19/gchq-intercepted-emails-journalists-ny-times-bbc-guardian-le-monde-reuters-nbc-washington-post?CMP=EMCNEWEML6619I2.

27 See Ball, 'GCHQ captured emails of journalists'.

28 See R. A. Clarke, M. J. Morell, G. R. Stone, C. R. Sunstein and P. Swire, *The NSA Report: Liberty and Security in a Changing World* (Princeton: Princeton University Press, 2014). This is reviewed, along with Glenn Greenwald's *No Place to Hide*, in D. Lyon, 'Big brother is listening to you: for your own good of course', *Books & Culture*, Nov.–Dec. 2014.

29 See Clarke et al., *The NSA Report*, p. xviii.

30 See 'Zeid appeals to Saudi Arabia to stop flogging of blogger', United Nations Human Rights, 15 Jan. 2015, at http://www. ohchr.org/FR/NewsEvents/Pages/DisplayNews.aspx?NewsID =15485&LangID=E.

31 See, for example, the work of O. Gandy, *Coming to Terms with Chance: Engaging Rational Discrimination and Cumulative Disadvantage* (Farnham, UK: Ashgate, 2009).

32 See K. Milberry and A. Clement, 'Policing as spectacle and the politics of surveillance at the Toronto G20', in M. Beare, N. des Rosiers and A. C. Deshman (eds), *Putting the State on Trial* (Vancouver: UBC Press, 2015).

33 See e.g. TVO journalist and TV host Steve Paikin. See R. Brennan, 'Toronto journalist witnessed "police brutality" at Toronto G20', Thestar.com, 6 Dec. 2010, at http://www.thestar. com/news/gta/g20/2010/12/06/toronto_journalist_witnessed _police_brutality_at_toronto_g20.html/.

34 See e.g. E. Stoddart, *Theological Perspectives on a Surveillance Society* (London: Ashgate, 2012), p. 51.

35 See Editorial board, 'Edward Snowden: whistle-blower', *New York Times*, 1 Jan. 2014, at http://www.nytimes.com/2014/01/02/ opinion/edward-snowden-whistle-blower.html?_r=0/.

36 See Pen American Center, *Chilling Effects: NSA Surveillance Drives Writers to Self-Censor*, research by the FDR Group, PEN International, 12 Nov. 2013, at http://www.pen-international. org/read-pen-american-centres-report-chilling-effects-nsa -surveillance-drives-writers-to-self-censor/. PEN is a writers' organization, founded in the UK in 1926 to defend freedom of expression.

37 See K. Hampton, L. Rainie, W. Lu, M. Dwyer, I. Shin and K. Purcell, *Social Media and the 'Spiral of Silence'*, Pew Research Internet Project, 26 Aug. 2014, at http://www.pewinternet. org/2014/08/26/social-media-and-the-spiral-of-silence/ #fn-11806-1/.

38 See H. Arendt, *Totalitarianism: Part Three of The Origins of Totalitarianism* (New York: Harcourt, Brace & World, 1968), p. 124.

39 See D. Priest and W. M. Arkin, 'Top secret America: a *Washington Post* investigation', *Washington Post*, 10 Sept. 2010, at http://projects.washingtonpost.com/top-secret-america/.

40 See H. Arendt, *Eichmann in Jerusalem: A Report on the Banality of Evil* (New York: Viking, 1963).

41 See J. Rancière, 'Democracy, republic, representation', *Constellations* 13.3 (2006): 297–307; cited in A. M. Brighenti, *Visibility in Social Theory and Social Research* (London: Palgrave Macmillan, 2010), p. 184.

42 See K. D. Haggerty and M. Samatas (eds), *Surveillance and Democracy* (London: Routledge, 2010).

43 See e.g. S. Wolin, *Democracy Incorporated: Managed Democracy and the Specter of Inverted Totalitarianism* (Princeton: Princeton University Press, 2010).

44 See K. Breckenridge and S. Szreter (eds), *Registration and Recognition: Documenting the Person in World History* (Oxford: Oxford University Press, 2012).

45 See E. Pariser, *The Filter Bubble: What the Internet Is Hiding from You* (New York: Penguin, 2011).

46 Agamben traces this back to François Quesnay (1694–1774), who went beyond the absolute monarch's care for citizen security and established security (sureté) as the central notion in the theory of government, especially in famine. Previously, the strategy was to prevent famine by creating public granaries and forbidding cereal export. But this damaged production. Quesnay's solution was to reverse policy: let famine happen and take control of its consequences. G. Agamben, 'For a theory of destituent power', lecture in Athens, 16 Nov. 2013, at http://www.chronosmag.eu/index.php/g-agamben-for-a-theory-of-destituent-power.html.

47 See L. Zedner, *Security* (London: Routledge, 2009), p. 11.

48 Zedner, *Security*, p. 12.

49 Clarke et al., *The NSA Report*.

50 Clarke et al., *The NSA Report*, p. xvii.

51 See e.g. D. Solove, *Nothing to Hide: The False Tradeoff between Privacy and Security* (New Haven: Yale University Press, 2012).

52 See D. Garland, *The Culture of Control: Crime and Social Order in Contemporary Society* (Chicago: University of Chicago Press, 2002).

Chapter 5 Framing Futures

Epigraph: Interview with Alan Rusbridger and Ewen MacAskill, see 'Edward Snowden interview – the edited transcript', *The Guardian*, 18 July 2014, at http://www.theguardian.com/world/2014/jul/18/-sp-edward-snowden-nsa-whistleblower-interview-transcript/.

1 See 'Edward Snowden delivers Channel 4's alternative Christmas message', news release, 4 Press, 24 Dec. 2013, at http://www.channel4.com/info/press/news/edward-snowden-delivers-channel-4s-alternative-christmas-message/.

2 See M. Schoenhals, *Spying for the People: Mao's Secret Agents 1949–1965* (Cambridge: Cambridge University Press, 2013).

3 See G. Lovell, 'The archive that never was: state terror and historical memory in Guatemala', *Geographical Review* 103.2 (2013): 199–209.

4 See A. Dorfman, 'Repression by any other name', *Guernica*, 3 Feb. 2014, at https://www.guernicamag.com/features/repression-by-any-other-name/.

5 International Civil Liberties Monitoring Group, *Report of the Information Clearinghouse on Border Controls and Infringements to Travellers' Rights*, Ottawa, 2010, at http://www.travelwatchlist.ca/updir/travelwatchlist/ICLMG_Watchlists_Report.pdf.

6 See D. Mosbergen, 'George Orwell's "1984" book sales sky-rocket in wake of NSA surveillance scandal', *Huffington Post*, 11 June 2013, at http://www.huffingtonpost.com/2013/06/11/orwell-1984-sales_n_3423185.html/.

7 See D. Solove, *The Digital Person: Technology and Privacy in the Information Age* (New York: New York University Press, 2004), ch. 3.

8 See D. Eggers, *The Circle* (New York: Vintage, 2013).
9 See D. Lyon, paper given at Surveillance Studies Network conference, Barcelona, 2014.
10 The phrase 'finding a balance between privacy and security' is routinely intoned by governments and media alike but it is at best vacuous and at worst a cloak for undermining the one to bolster the other.
11 See e.g. the call to consider the importance of 'inherent and strategic values' of privacy, that distinguish private and public lives and enable the exercise of other social and political rights, from political scientist Charles Raab in 'Privacy as a security value', in D. W. Schartum, L. Bygrave and A. G. B. Bekken (eds), *Jon Bing: En Hyllest / A Tribute* (Oslo: Gyldendal, 2014), pp. 39–58.
12 See e.g. D. Broeders, 'The public core of the internet: an international agenda for internet governance', WRR-Policy Brief no. 2, WRR (The Netherlands Scientific Council for Government Policy), The Hague, April 2015.
13 See e.g. academic journals that deal with ethical issues of surveillance such as *Ethics and Information Technology* (Springer) and *Journal of Information, Communication, and Ethics in Society* (Emerald).
14 See K. Ball and L. Snider (eds), *The Surveillance-Industrial Complex: Towards a Political Economy of Surveillance* (London: Routledge, 2014).
15 See A. Narayanan and S. Vallor, 'Why software engineering courses should include ethics coverage', *Communications of the ACM* 57.3 (2014): 23–5.
16 See J. Ginsberg et al., 'Detecting influenza epidemics using search engine query data', *Nature* 457 (2009): 1012–14, at http://www.nature.com/nature/journal/v457/n7232/full/nature07634.html; D. Lazer, R. Kennedy, G. King and A. Vespignani, 'The parable of Google flu: traps in big data analysis', *Science* 343.6176 (2014): 1203–5, at http://www.sciencemag.org/content/343/6176/1203.
17 Of course, actually creating ubiquitous and continuous coverage is as implausible today as in Orwell's time. But what the NSA leaks show is that there's always the nagging possibility of

surveillance. Uncertainty fosters fear, which creates compliance. A system that sounds as if it cares about people – 'it's for security against terrorism' – actually controls through uncertainty and fear.

18 See 'George Orwell under the watchful eye of Big Brother', Freedom of Information release, National Archives, at http://www.nationalarchives.gov.uk/releases/2005/highlights_july/july19/default.htm.

19 See R. Williams, *Orwell* (London: Fontana, 1971), p. 78.

20 K. Nursall, 'Canadian authors join world-wide condemnation of mass surveillance', *Toronto Star*, 12 Dec. 2013, at http://www.thestar.com/entertainment/2013/12/10/canadian_authors_join_worldwide_condemnation_of_mass_surveillance.html.

21 See e.g. Bennett, *The Privacy Advocates: Resisting the Spread of Surveillance* (Cambridge MA: MIT Press, 2008).

22 See D. Lyon, 'Surveillance, Snowden and big data: capacities, consequences, critique', *Big Data & Society* 1.1 (2014), at http://bds.sagepub.com/content/1/2/2053951714541861.abstract/.

23 See R. Levitas, *Utopia as Method: The Imaginary Reconstitution of Society* (London: Palgrave Macmillan, 2013), p. xi.

24 See N. Wolterstorff, *Journey toward Justice: Personal Encounters in the Global South* (Grand Rapids, MI: Baker Academic, 2013), p. 48.

25 The term is from Eric Stoddart, *Theological Perspectives on a Surveillance Society* (London: Ashgate, 2012). Nicholas Wolterstorff also sees agapic love as 'care' (*Journey toward Justice*, p. 110). Such love is shown in both the concern for the other's well-being and simultaneously in showing respect for the other, due to her or his worth. Rights, says Wolterstorff, represent an interweaving of these two, well-being and worth (or dignity). This also demonstrates the connection between love as 'care about' and justice. To seek justice is to show love. Exploring such aspects of care in relation to surveillance practices would be an effective starting point in counteracting the effects of the kind of cybernetic management control that deflects attention from relational-ethical criteria and that characterizes much surveillance today.

26 See Q. Hardy, 'They have seen the future of the internet, and it is dark', Bits, 5 July 2014, at http://bits.blogs.nytimes. com/2014/07/05/they-have-seen-the-future-of-the-internet -and-it-is-dark/?_php=true&_type=blogs&emc=edit_th_20140 706&nl=todaysheadlines&nlid=55961761&_r=0.

27 See L. Amoore, 'Security and the incalculable', *Security Dialogue* 45.5 (2014): 423–39; Stoddart, *Theological Perspectives on a Surveillance Society*.

28 D. Lyon, *Surveillance Studies: An Overview* (Cambridge: Polity, 2007); L. Zedner, *Security* (London: Routledge, 2009), p. 80.

29 The parallel in consumer surveillance is what I term 'categorical seduction', Lyon, *Surveillance Studies*.

30 See Zedner, *Security*.

31 See R. Raley 'Dataveillance and countervailance', in L. Gitelman (ed.), *"Raw Data" Is an Oxymoron* (Cambridge, MA: MIT Press, 2013), p. 128.

32 V. Meyer-Schoenberger, *Delete: The Virtue of Forgetting in the Digital Age* (Princeton: Princeton University Press, 2010).

33 See 'Canadians' mental-health info routinely shared with FBI, U.S. Customs', *CBC News*, 14 Apr. 2014, at http://www.cbc.ca/ news/canada/windsor/canadians-mental-health-info -routinely-shared-with-fbi-u-s-customs-1.2609159.

34 See Narayanan and Vallor, 'Why software engineering courses should include ethics coverage'.

35 See C. Taylor, *A Secular Age* (Cambridge, MA: Harvard University Press, 2007), p. 161.

36 See A. Sayer, *Why Things Matter to People: Social Science, Values and Ethical Life* (Cambridge: Cambridge University Press, 2011).

37 Snowden's emphasis is on the need for choices to be made. If pressed, I suspect that he would acknowledge the ambivalence of terms such as 'control' or 'freedom' and the fact that both are found in the very structure of the internet.

38 The vision that inspires me sees framing as crucial. For instance, pitting 'privacy' values such as individual self-determination against technological mastery seen in surveillance software is

inadequate. In principle, both the desire for personal freedom and the freedom to improve technological systems may be viewed as ethically permissible, if not praiseworthy. This is why a wider context is required, one that seeks for the fruits of justice to be enjoyed by all, in relationships of peace. Theologically, this is explained in N. Wolterstorff, *Until Justice and Peace Embrace* (Grand Rapids, MI: Eerdmans, 1983), pp. 69–72.

39 Information about specific organizations concerned with practical policy matters may be found through privacy and information commissions, civil liberties associations and other agencies. Some are listed in C. Bennett et al., *Transparent Lives: Surveillance in Canada* (also *Vivre à nu. La surveillance au Canada*) (Edmonton: Athabasca University Press, 2014).

40 Coalitions against mass surveillance have engaged in several concerted global events since Snowden's disclosures began. See e.g. Y. Welinder, 'Global action against mass surveillance on the anniversary of the Snowden revelations', Wikimedia blog, 5 June 2014, at https://blog.wikimedia.org/2014/06/05/global-action-against-mass-surveillance-snowden-revelations/. The 'transparency' question, however, is in tension with the legitimate but limited need for secrecy within intelligence agencies. Research could fruitfully be brought to bear on this vexed question.

SELECTED BIBLIOGRAPHY

Agamben, G., 'For a theory of destituent power', *Chronos.* Public lecture in Athens, 16 Nov. 2013. At http://www. chronosmag.eu/index.php/g-agamben-for-a-theory-of -destituent-power.html.

Al Jazeera, 'Timeline of Edward Snowden revelations'. Al Jazeera America, 2015. At http://america.aljazeera.com/ articles/multimedia/timeline-edward-snowden-revela tions.html/.

Altheide, D., 'The triumph of fear: connecting the dots about whistleblowers and surveillance', *International Journal of Cyber Warfare and Terrorism* 4.1 (2014): 1–7.

Arendt, H., *Eichmann in Jerusalem: A Report on the Banality of Evil.* New York: Viking, 1963.

Arendt, H., *Totalitarianism: Part Three of The Origins of Totalitarianism.* New York: Harcourt, Brace & World, 1968.

Assange, J., *When Google Met WikiLeaks.* New York: OR Books, 2014.

Ball, K. and Snider, L. (eds), *The Surveillance-Industrial Complex: Towards a Political Economy of Surveillance*. London: Routledge, 2014.

Ball, K. S. and Webster, F., *The Intensification of Surveillance*. London: Pluto Press, 2003.

Bauman, Z. and Lyon, D., *Liquid Surveillance: A Conversation*. Cambridge: Polity, 2013.

Bauman, Z., Bigo, D., Esteves, P., Guild, E., Jabri, V., Lyon, D. and Walker, R. B., 'After Snowden: rethinking the impact of surveillance', *International Political Sociology* 8.2 (2014): 121–44.

Bennett, C. J., *The Privacy Advocates: Resisting the Spread of Surveillance*. Cambridge, MA: MIT Press, 2008.

Bennett, C., 'In defence of privacy: the concept and the regime', *Surveillance & Society* 8.4 (2011): 485–96. At http://library.queensu.ca/ojs/index.php/surveillance-and -society/article/view/4184/4186/.

Bennett, C. and Raab, C., *The Governance of Privacy: Policy Instruments in Global Perspective*. Cambridge, MA: MIT Press, 2006.

Bennett, C., Haggerty, K., Lyon, D. and Steeves, V. (eds), *Transparent Lives: Surveillance in Canada* (also *Vivre à nu. La surveillance au Canada)*. Edmonton: Athabasca University Press, 2014. At http://www.aupress.ca/index.php/ books/120237.

Bigo, D., 'Globalized (in)security: the field and the banopticon', in D. Bigo and A. Tsouskala (eds), *Terror, Insecurity and Liberty*. London: Routledge, 2008.

Bok, S., *Secrets: The Ethics of Concealment and Revelation*. New York: Vintage, 1989.

boyd, d. and Crawford, K., 'Critical questions for big data: provocations for a cultural, technological, and scholarly phenomenon', *Information, Communication & Society* 15.5 (2012): 662–79.

Breckenridge, K. and Szreter, S. (eds), *Registration and Recognition: Documenting the Person in World History*. Oxford: Oxford University Press, 2012.

Brodeur, J. P., *The Policing Web*. Oxford: Oxford University Press, 2010.

Campbell, D. and Connor, S., *On the Record: Surveillance, Computers and Privacy*. London: Michael Joseph, 1986.

Castells, M., *The Rise of the Network Society*, vol. 1 of *The Information Age: Economy, Society and Culture*. Oxford: Blackwell, 1996; 2nd edn 2000.

Castells, M., *The Power of Identity*, vol. 2 of *The Information Age: Economy, Society and Culture*. Oxford: Blackwell, 1997; 2nd edn 2004.

Castells, M., *End of Millennium*, vol. 3 of *The Information Age: Economy, Society and Culture*. Oxford: Blackwell, 1998; 2nd edn 2000.

Castells, M., *The Internet Galaxy*. Oxford: Oxford University Press, 2001.

Castells, M., *Communication Power*. Oxford: Oxford University Press, 2009.

Clarke, R. A., Morell, M. J., Stone, G. R., Sunstein, C. R. and Swire, P., *The NSA Report: Liberty and Security in a Changing World*. Princeton: Princeton University Press, 2014.

Clement, A., 'Canada's bad dream', *World Policy Journal* (Fall 2014). At http://www.worldpolicy.org/journal/fall2014/canada%27s-bad-dream/.

Cohen, J., *Configuring the Networked Self: Law, Code, and the Play of Everyday Practice*. New Haven: Yale University Press, 2012.

Cohen, S., *Visions of Social Control*. Cambridge: Polity, 2012.

Coleman, G., *Hacker, Hoaxer, Whistleblower, Spy: The Many Faces of Anonymous*. London: Verso, 2014.

Dandeker, C., *Surveillance, Power and Modernity*. Cambridge: Polity, 1990.

Deibert, R., *Black Code: Surveillance, Privacy and the Dark Side of the Internet*. Toronto: Signal, 2013.

de Sola Pool, I., *Technologies of Freedom*. Cambridge, MA: Harvard University Press, 1983.

Dorfman, A., 'Repression by any other name', *Guernica*, 3 Feb. 2014. At https://www.guernicamag.com/features/repression-by-any-other-name/.

Edwards, P., *Closed Worlds: Computers and the Politics of Discourse in Cold War America*. Cambridge, MA: MIT Press, 1996.

Eggers, D., *The Circle*. New York: Vintage, 2013.

Ellul, J., *The Technological Society*. New York: Vintage, 1967.

Fieschi, C., 'The social value of privacy', in C. Edwards and C. Fieschi (eds), *UK Confidential*. London: Demos, 2008. At http://www.demos.co.uk/files/UK%20confidential%20-%20web.pdf.

Fidler, D. P. (ed.), *The Snowden Reader*. Bloomington: Indiana University Press, 2015.

Fuchs, C., 'Critique of the political economy of Web 2.0 surveillance', in C. Fuchs, K. Boersma, A. Albrechtslund and M. Sandova (eds), *Internet and Surveillance: Challenges of Web 2.0 and Social Media*. London: Routledge, 2012.

Fuchs, C., *Social Media: A Critical Introduction*. London: Sage, 2014.

Fuchs, C., Boersma, K., Albrechtslund, A. and Sandoval, M. (eds), *Internet and Surveillance: Challenges of Web 2.0 and Social Media*. London: Routledge, 2012.

Gandy, O. H., Jr, *Coming to Terms with Chance: Engaging Rational Discrimination and Cumulative Disadvantage*. Farnham, UK: Ashgate, 2009.

Garland, D., *The Culture of Control: Crime and Social Order in Contemporary Society*. Chicago: University of Chicago Press, 2002.

Geist, M. (ed.), *Law, Privacy and Surveillance in Canada in the Post-Snowden Era*, Ottawa: University of Ottawa Press, 2015. Available under a Creative Commons licence at http://www.ruor.uottawa.ca/handle/10393/32 424/.

Gerovitch, S., 'The cybernetics scare and the origins of the internet', *Baltic Worlds* 11.1 (2010): 32–8. At http://baltic worlds.com/the-cybernetics-scare-and-the-origins-of -the-internet/.

Gibson, W., 'Burning Chrome', *Omni*, July 1982.

Gibson, W., *Neuromancer*. New York: Ace, 1984.

Giroux, H., 'Totalitarian paranoia in the post-Orwellian surveillance state', *Cultural Studies*, online 14 May 2014. At http://dx.doi.org/10.1080/09502386.2014.917118.

Greenwald. G., *No Place to Hide: Edward Snowden, the NSA, and the US Surveillance State*. New York: Metropolitan Books; Toronto: Signal, 2014.

Haggerty, K. and Ericson, R., *Policing the Risk Society*. Toronto: University of Toronto Press, 1997.

Haggerty, K. and Ericson, R., 'The surveillant assemblage', *British Journal of Sociology* 51.4 (2000): 605–22.

Haggerty, K. D. and Samatas, M. (eds), *Surveillance and Democracy*. London: Routledge, 2010.

Hampton, K., Rainie, L., Lu, W., Dwyer, M., Shin, I. and Purcell, K., *Social Media and the 'Spiral of Silence'*. Pew Research Internet Project, 26 Aug. 2014. At http://www. pewinternet.org/2014/08/26/social-media-and-the -spiral-of-silence/#fn-11806-1/.

Hand, M., *Making Digital Cultures*. London: Ashgate, 2008.

Harris, S., *The Watchers: The Rise of America's Surveillance State*. London: Penguin, 2013.

Innis, H. A., *The Bias of Communication*. Toronto: University of Toronto Press, 1962.

Keizer, G., *Privacy*. New York: Picador, 2012.

Kitchin, R., *The Data Revolution: Big Data, Open Data, Data Infrastructures and Their Consequences*. London: Sage, 2014.

Kitchin, R., 'Thinking critically about and researching algorithms'. Social Science Research Network, 28 Oct. 2014. At http://papers.ssrn.com/sol3/papers.cfm?abstract_id=2515786.

Kraemer, F., van Overveld, K. and Peterson, M., 'Is there an ethics of algorithms?', *Ethics of Information Technology* 13 (2011): 251–60.

Larsen, E., *The Naked Consumer: How Our Private Lives Become Public Commodities*. New York: Penguin Books, 1994.

Levitas, R., *Utopia as Method: The Imaginary Reconstitution of Society*. London: Palgrave Macmillan, 2013.

Lovell, G., 'The archive that never was: state terror and historical memory in Guatemala', *Geographical Review* 103.2 (2013): 199–209.

Lyon, D., *The Information Society: Issues and Illusions*. Cambridge: Polity, 1988.

Lyon, D., *The Electronic Eye: The Rise of the Surveillance Society*. Cambridge: Polity, 1994.

Lyon, D., *Surveillance Society: Monitoring Everyday Life*. Buckingham, UK: Open University Press, 2001.

Lyon, D., *Surveillance after September 11*. Cambridge: Polity, 2003.

Lyon, D. (ed.), *Surveillance as Social Sorting: Privacy, Risk and Digital Discrimination*. London: Routledge, 2003.

Lyon, D., 'A sociology of information', in C. Calhoun, C. Rojek and B. Turner (eds), *The Sage Handbook of Sociology*. London: Sage, 2005, pp. 222–35.

Lyon, D., *Surveillance Studies: An Overview*. Cambridge: Polity, 2007.

Lyon, D., 'Being post-secular in the social sciences: Taylor's social imaginaries', *New Blackfriars* 91 (2010): 648–62.

Lyon, D., 'The emerging surveillance culture', in A. Jansson and M. Christiansen (eds), *Media, Surveillance and Identity*. New York: Peter Lang, 2014, pp. 71–88.

Lyon, D., 'Surveillance and the eye of God', *Studies in Christian Ethics* 27.1 (2014): 1–12.

Lyon, D., 'Surveillance, Snowden and big data: capacities, consequences, critique', *Big Data & Society* 1.1 (2014). At http://bds.sagepub.com/content/1/2/2053951714541861.abstract/.

Lyon, D. and Topak, Ö., 'Promoting global identification: corporations, IGOs and ID card systems', in K. Ball and L. Snider (eds), *The Surveillance-Industrial Complex: Towards a Political Economy of Surveillance*. London: Routledge, 2014, pp. 27–43.

Marquez, X., 'Spaces of appearance and spaces of surveillance', *Polity* 44 (2012): 6–31.

Marquis-Boire, M., 'Schrodinger's cat video and the death of clear-text', Citizen Lab, Research Brief 46, 15 Aug. 2014. At https://citizenlab.org/2014/08/cat-video-and-the-death-of-clear-text/.

Marwick, A., 'The public domain: social surveillance in everyday life', *Surveillance & Society* 9.4 (2012): 378–93. At http://library.queensu.ca/ojs/index.php/surveillance-and-society/article/viewFile/pub_dom/pub_dom/.

Marwick, A., *Status Update: Celebrity, Publicity and Branding in the Social Media Age*. New Haven: Yale University Press, 2013.

Marx, G., *Undercover: Police Surveillance in America*. Berkeley: University of California Press, 1988.

Mayer, J., 'The secret sharer', *New Yorker*, 23 May 2011. At http://www.newyorker.com/magazine/2011/05/23/the-secret-sharer/.

Menzies, H., 'Digital networks: the medium of communication, and the message', *Canadian Journal of*

Communication 24.4 (1999). At http://www.cjc-online.ca/index.php/journal/article/view/1125/1033/.

Mosco, V., *To the Cloud: Big Data in a Turbulent World*. Boulder, CO: Paradigm, 2014.

Murakami Wood, D. (ed.), *A Report on the Surveillance Society*. Wilmslow, UK: Office of the Information Commissioner, 2006. Summary report at https://ico.org.uk/media/about -the-ico/documents/1042391/surveillance-society-sum mary-06.pdf.

Murakami Wood, D. and Ball, K., 'Brandscapes of control? Surveillance, marketing and the co-construction of subjectivity and space in neo-liberal capitalism', *Marketing Theory* 13.1 (2013): 47–67.

9-11 Commission, *The 9/11 Commission Report*. National Commission on Terrorist Attacks upon the United States, 2004. At http://govinfo.library.unt.edu/911/report/.

Nissenbaum, H., *Privacy in Context: Technology, Policy and the Integrity of Social Life*. Stanford: Stanford Law Books, 2009.

Pariser, E., *The Filter Bubble: What the Internet Is Hiding from You*. New York: Penguin, 2011.

Pen American Center, *Chilling Effects: NSA Surveillance Drives Writers to Self-Censor*, research by the FDR Group, PEN International, 12 Nov. 2013. At http://www.pen -international.org/read-pen-american-centres-report -chilling-effects-nsa-surveillance-drives-writers-to-self -censor/.

Poitras, L. (dir.), *Citizenfour*. Documentary film produced by L. Poitras, M. Bonnefoy and D. Wilutzky, 2014.

Regan, P., *Legislating Privacy: Technology, Social Values and Public Policy* (1995). Durham: University of North Carolina Press, 2009.

Savage, M., 'Digital fields, networks and capital: sociology beyond structures and fluids', in K. Orton-Johnson and

N. Prior (eds), *Digital Sociology: Critical Perspectives*. Basingstoke, UK: Palgrave Macmillan, 2013, pp. 139–50.

Sayer, A., *Why Things Matter to People: Social Science, Values and Ethical Life*. Cambridge: Cambridge University Press, 2011.

Schiller, D., 'How to think about information', in V. Mosco and J. Wasko (eds), *The Political Economy of Information*. Madison: University of Wisconsin Press, 1988, pp. 27–44.

Schoenhals, M., *Spying for the People: Mao's Secret Agents 1949–1965*. Cambridge: Cambridge University Press, 2013.

Smist, F. J., Jr, *Congress Oversees the United States Intelligence Community, 1947–1989*. Knoxville: University of Tennessee Press, 1990.

Snowden Digital Surveillance Archive. Project partners: Canadian Journalists for Free Expression (CJFE) and the Politics of Surveillance Project at the Faculty of Information at the University of Toronto, 2015. At https://snowdenarchive.cjfe.org/greenstone/cgi-bin/library.cgi.

Solove, D., *The Digital Person: Technology and Privacy in the Information Age*. New York: New York University Press, 2004.

Solove, D., *Nothing to Hide: The False Tradeoff between Privacy and Security*. New Haven: Yale University Press, 2012.

Steeves, V., 'Reclaiming the social value of privacy', in I. Kerr, C. Lucock and V. Steeves (eds), *Lessons from the Identity Trail: Anonymity, Privacy and Identity in a Networked Age*. Oxford: Oxford University Press, 2009.

Steeves, V., *Young Canadians in a Wired World, Phase III: Online Privacy, Online Publicity*. Ottawa: MediaSmarts, 2014. At http://mediasmarts.ca/sites/mediasmarts/files/pdfs/publication-report/full/YCWWIII_Online_Privacy_Online_Publicity_FullReport.pdf/.

Stoddart, E., *Theological Perspectives on a Surveillance Society*. London: Ashgate, 2012.

Taylor, C., *A Secular Age*. Cambridge, MA: Harvard University Press, 2007.

Taylor, E., *Surveillance Schools: Security, Discipline and Control in Contemporary Education*. London: Macmillan, 2013.

Trottier, D., *Social Media as Surveillance: Rethinking Visibility in a Converging World*. London: Ashgate, 2012.

Trottier, D. and Lyon, D., 'Key features of social media surveillance', in C. Fuchs, K. Boersma, A. Albrechtslund and M. Sandoval (eds), *Internet and Surveillance: Challenges of Web 2.0 and Social Media*. London: Routledge, 2012.

Williams, R., *Orwell*. London: Fontana, 1971.

Wolin, S., *Democracy Incorporated: Managed Democracy and the Specter of Inverted Totalitarianism*. Princeton: Princeton University Press, 2010.

Wolterstorff, N., *Journey toward Justice: Personal Encounters in the Global South*. Grand Rapids, MI: Baker Academic, 2013.

Zedner, L., *Security*. London: Routledge, 2009.

Zureik, E., 'The cross-cultural study of privacy', in E. Zureik, L. Harling Stalker, E. Smith, D. Lyon and Y. E. Chan (eds), *Surveillance, Privacy and the Globalization of Personal Information*. Montreal and Kingston: McGill-Queen's University Press, 2010.

INDEX